THE HOLOCAUST AND THE HENMAID'S TALE

THE HOLOCAUST
AND THE HENMAID'S TALE

A Case for Comparing Atrocities

Karen Davis, PhD

Lantern Books • New York
A Division of Booklight Inc.

2005
Lantern Books
One Union Square West, Suite 201
New York, NY 10003

Printed in the United States of America

Library of Congress Cataloging-in-Publication Data

Davis, Karen, 1944–
The Holocaust and the henmaid's tale : a case for comparing atrocities /
Karen Davis.
p. cm.
Includes bibliographical references and index.
ISBN 1-59056-091-4 (alk. paper)
1. Animal welfare. 2. Holocaust, Jewish (1939-1945) I. Title.
HV4708.D36 2005
179'.1—dc22
                                        2005013691

This book is dedicated to all the soft and innocent lives

who are at our mercy.

TABLE OF CONTENTS

ACKNOWLEDGMENTS

While this book is the result of many varied and diverse influences, conscious and otherwise, certain people and organizations have made specific and indispensable contributions to the writing and production of it. I wish to thank them at this time.

My gratitude goes to:

The editors of *Best Friends* magazine, who planted the seed of inquiry by asking me whether I thought comparing the treatment of animals raised and slaughtered for food with the Holocaust "went too far."

Daniel Ziskin and Philip Schein, who directed me in the initial stages of writing to some of the important scholarship on the Holocaust and on the role of animals in the Jewish tradition.

Pattrice Jones, who commented helpfully on the first draft of what would ultimately become *The Holocaust and the Henmaid's Tale*.

The editors of the American Anti-Vivisection Society's *AV Magazine*, who asked me to write an essay on the life and death of the "battery" hen.

Mike Zeliff, who on hearing my description of how hens are treated by the egg industry said that it reminded him of Margaret Atwood's dystopian novel *The Handmaid's Tale*, whereupon the title of this book was born.

Matt Prescott, the creator of the Holocaust on Your Plate exhibit for People for the Ethical Treatment of Animals, who via personal communication provided me with much valuable information about the genesis and goal of the exhibit.

Roberta Kalechofsky, who clarified via personal communication certain aspects of Jewish opposition to comparisons between animal suffering and the Holocaust.

Sean Day, who provided me with the court case cited in endnote 9 on the greater suffering that may be endured by an individual who cannot conceptualize the cause, compared to one who can.

Charles Patterson, whose landmark book *Eternal Treblinka* presents detailed evidence of the psychohistorical connections between the Holocaust and our species' horrible treatment of nonhuman animals in everyday life.

Steve Best, who gave judicious editing assistance with my article "A Tale of Two Holocausts," of which this book is the final product, in preparation for publishing the article in the third issue of his Center on Animal Liberation Affairs (cala.org) publication, *Animal Liberation Philosophy and Policy Studies Journal*.

Martin Rowe and Sarah Gallogly of Lantern Books, who graciously chose to publish *The Holocaust and the Henmaid's Tale* based on their belief that this book is a valuable contribution to the discipline of Holocaust and animal studies.

PREFACE

Blurring the Boundary between Human and Nonhuman Beings

Heinrich Himmler, who founded the quasi-military police unit known as the SS and administered the Nazi death camps, was initially a chicken farmer. According to Charles Patterson, in his book *Eternal Treblinka: Our Treatment of Animals and the Holocaust*, Himmler's "agricultural studies and experience breeding chickens convinced him that since all behavioral characteristics are hereditary, the most effective way to shape the future of a population—human or non-human—was to institute breeding projects that favored the desirable and eliminated the undesirable" (100).

"By blurring the boundary between animals and human beings," says Boria Sax in his book *Animals in the Third Reich: Pets, Scapegoats, and the Holocaust*, "many Nazi practices made the killing of people seem like the slaughtering of animals. The Nazis forced those whom they were about to murder to get completely undressed and huddle together, something that is not normal behavior for human beings. Nakedness suggests an identity as animals; when combined with crowding, it suggests a herd of cattle or sheep" (150)—or, as well, a pile of defeathered chickens. Their resemblance to animals, particularly those raised for food, "made the victims easier to shoot or gas."

For most commentators, blurring the boundary between

humans and nonhumans in order to harm humans more easily is disturbing, not because it raises questions about how we treat nonhuman beings, but because it threatens our superior status as humans. For many people, the idea that it is as morally wrong to harm animals intentionally as it is to harm humans intentionally borders on heresy. Similarly, the idea that animals could suffer as terribly as humans in being forced into unnatural patterns of behavior (ethologist Konrad Lorenz said, for example, that forcing hens to lay their eggs in crowded cages is as instinctively humiliating for them as it is for humans to be forced to defecate in front of one another) threatens age-old assumptions that animals exist for us to manipulate as we see fit. Hostility between and among human groups is an integral part of our history, but just as bickering individuals and nations come together against a common enemy, so people, by and large, are united in defense of human supremacy over all other forms of life. The boundary between "human" and "animal" is kept clear.

In reality, however, the boundary is continuously blurred. Theriomorphy, in which the human and nonhuman animal comes together, takes many forms. Human and nonhuman animals share a common evolutionary heritage and sentience, and we share many similar and identical interests and behaviors. Meateaters incorporate animals into themselves by eating them, human infants' first milk is often that of a lactating cow or goat, and many people are theriomorphic as a result of cross-species organ transplantations. So-called bestiality—sexual relations involving human and nonhuman animals—is, as Midas Dekkers observes in his book *Dearest Pet: On Bestiality*, "omnipresent—in art, in science, in history, in our dreams" (5).

In myth and religion, animals are frequently employed by the gods to impregnate women. In this regard, Dekkers writes, "Jesus Christ, himself the Lamb of God, had absolutely no need to be ashamed of his origins, since the dove which had fathered him in Mary was a god as well as a dove. Like the children of Leda and her swan [in Greek mythology], he is at the same time the product of bestiality (man x animal) and of theogamy (god x man). The same ambiguity is found in other religions" (10).

A similar ambiguity appears in Western science. Animals are substituted for humans in biomedical research, which is based on the assumption that animals can double for people as sources of information about the human condition. Inflicting human diseases on animals in search of a cure, however modern this may seem, is essentially a type of primitive purification ritual. Through the ages, people have sought consciously or unconsciously to rid themselves of their impurities (diseases, sins, and vices) by symbolically transferring their impurities to sacrificial victims, known as scapegoats. Often, these victims are represented as having both human and nonhuman attributes. In Christianity, Jesus is the sacrificial lamb who bears away the sins of the world. In the Hasidic custom of kaparos (atonements), adherents transfer their sins symbolically to chickens, their "doubles," who are then slaughtered. Swinging a chicken three times by the legs around his or her head, the practitioner chants: "This is my exchange, this is my substitute, this is my atonement. This chicken shall go to its death, and I shall proceed to a good, long life and peace" (Wenig, 2).

The ritual transference of one's own transgressions and diseases to a sacrificial animal victim constitutes an interspecies rape of that victim. In both cases, the animal victim is treated as a receptacle for the victimizer's defilement. In both cases, the animal victim is involuntarily made to appear as an aspect of the victimizer's identity. Humans, by virtue of a shared verbal language, can aggressively challenge the profanation and misappropriation of their identity. By contrast, a nonhuman animal, such as a hen, is powerless, short of human intercession, to protect her identity from being besmirched, as when she is represented by her abusers as an "egg-laying machine," or as a symbolic uterus for the deposition of a human being's spiritual filth, illustrating Jim Mason's observation, in his book *An Unnatural Order: Uncovering the Roots of Our Domination of Nature and Each Other*, that traditional religion "sets up a mind that is 'entertained' by scenes of debasement" (180).

The boundary between animals as food and animals as sexual objects is blurred, even though most people conventionally view animals as food in a wholesome, utilitarian light. Even so, the rape of farmed animals is an age-old practice, and not only because these animals are readily available for sexual assault (Dekkers, 133–138; Beirne; Davis 2001a, 13–14). Farmed-animal production is based on manipulating and controlling animals' sex lives and reproductive organs. Sexually abusive in essence, animal farming invites lascivious conduct and attitudes towards "food" animals on the part of producers and consumers alike—a fact exploited by advertisers who, for example, have used interspecies gang rape images to sell chicken "strips" to "the young adult male" customer (Espinosa).

In *The Sexual Politics of Meat* and *The Pornography of Meat*, feminist author Carol J. Adams has analyzed the relationship between the producing and consuming of animal products and pornographic attitudes towards women. In *An Unnatural Order*, Jim Mason links animal agriculture to encouragement of a deep-seated human desire to hurt and humiliate the bodies of other beings. In my book *More Than a Meal: The Turkey in History, Myth, Ritual, and Reality* (Davis 2001a), I discuss how the sexual politics of meat enter into modern turkey production and consumption. Why, I ask, are turkeys—the sacrificial victims of the national Thanksgiving holiday in America—not only slaughtered by the millions for the occasion, but also targeted for obscene media jokes surrounding the holiday each year?

Commenting on the sexual abuse of chickens, which "automatically involves sadism" and is "in many areas still so normal that it only gets into the papers when something goes wrong," Midas Dekkers writes suggestively of the perpetrators that '[s]ince animal abuse has been institutionalized in our society in the food industry, it cannot be difficult for such sadists to find satisfaction. Some of them are satisfied in an ordinary slaughterhouse" (136, 146–147). Consider this example of a man's sexual craving for pigs being slaughtered:

> C.L, 42 years of age, engineer. Remembers that in his boyhood he had enjoyed watching the slaughtering of domestic animals, and particularly of pigs. It often gave him a very strong sexual feeling and an ejaculation. Later he sought out slaughterhouses to enjoy watching the spurting blood and the death throes of the animals, which always gave him a mounting feeling of sexual pleasure (Dekkers, 147).

In his essay "Heavy Petting," philosopher Peter Singer says that a man raping a hen is horrifying because the cruelty of sexually penetrating a small bird is clear and simple. But, he inquires, "is it worse for the hen than living for a year or more crowded with four or five other hens in a barren wire cage so small that they can never stretch their wings, and then being stuffed into crates to be taken to the slaughterhouse, strung upside down on a conveyer belt and killed? If not, then it is no worse than what egg producers do to their hens all the time" (Singer 2001).

Asked in an interview whether he agreed with me that the manual milking and artificial insemination of turkeys in modern food production is an example of humanity's bestial behavior in areas normally regarded as sexless and innocuous,

Singer replied, "Yes. We draw the lines in strange places. That's what Karen's point is all about" (Vaughan, 8).

It is also very much what this book is about—the moral lines we draw, and why. The "henmaid" in the title of my book is an allusion to Margaret Atwood's dystopian novel, *The Handmaid's Tale*. In Atwood's novel, women are valued only if their ovaries are viable, and they are at the mercy of their keepers, their rapists—ordinary men controlling society with the help of female collaborators. When one day I was describing to a librarian how hens are treated by the egg industry, he said that it sounded chillingly like *The Handmaid's Tale*. As soon as he said this, the title of my book was born. The henmaid symbolizes the billions of birds who at this moment, and every moment, are imprisoned in the hell of the poultry and egg industry. More broadly, she symbolizes the innocent individuals of all species who suffer and die at our mercy.

Despite opposition by many, I believe that significant parallels can be drawn between the Holocaust and the institutionalized abuse of billions of nonhuman animals, and that there are lessons to be learned by viewing each of these evils through the bleak lens of the other. I believe there are similarities between the mentality of the Third Reich and the mentality of factory farming and vivisection, and I am not alone in my thinking. In *Animals in the Third Reich*, Boria Sax argues, for example, that "[t]he patterns we can observe in the Nazi treatment of animals may help to illuminate their attitudes toward human beings. At least on the level of conscious intent, the mentality of the Nazis was largely technocratic. This applies to the way in which they approached the slaughter of animals; it also applies to their mass murder of human beings. The ideal of the Nazis, especially of the SS, was to kill dispassionately without either cruelty or regret" (167).

In the modern world, the reduction of a sensitive being to a nonsentient object imprisoned in an excremental universe "outside of any moral universe of care," as Roberta Kalechofsky represents this nadir of existence in her book *Animal Suffering and the Holocaust: The Problem with Comparisons* (53), links the Holocaust victim to the animal victim in laboratories, factory farms, and slaughterhouses in ways that diminish the differences between them. Heinrich Himmler, the chicken farmer and Nazi executioner, epitomizes the pitiless spirit of human and nonhuman animal exploitation alike. For more than a decade in my work as founder and president of United Poultry Concerns, a nonprofit organization that addresses the treatment of chickens and other domestic fowl in all areas of their exploitation, I've encountered this pitiless spirit in farmed-animal industry publications and at the many industry conferences I've attended. To the leaders of the SS on October 4, 1943, Himmler blandly announced in a voice that is totally familiar to me:

> What happens to a Russian, to a Czech, does not interest me in the slightest. . . . Whether nations live in prosperity or starve to death interests me only in so far as we need them as slaves for our culture. . . . We shall never be rough or heartless when it is not necessary; that is clear. We Germans, who are the only people in the world who have a decent attitude toward animals, will also assume a decent attitude toward these human animals. But it is a crime against our own blood to worry about them (Sax, 167).

Let us turn then to consider this crime.

Chapter One

ONLY ONE HOLOCAUST?

Another scientist in Nazi Germany argued that there was a northern and a southern psychology which crossed the lines of species. To demonstrate this, he did a detailed study of chickens in various countries in the north and south of Europe. He observed such matters as the speed with which they picked up grain and the colors they responded to, and compared their mental profiles with the people who lived alongside them. The conclusion was that the "races" of chickens paralleled those of human beings.—**Boria Sax**, *Animals in the Third Reich*

As the Holocaust is sacralized, comparisons are perceived as blasphemy.—**Boria Sax**, *Animals in the Third Reich*

Holocaust victims WERE treated like animals, and so logically we can conclude that animals are treated like Holocaust victims.—**Matt Prescott**, creator of PETA's "Holocaust on Your Plate" campaign

They are being treated as if they were animals.
—International Red Cross Committee referring to prisoners in Iraq under American supervision

That there could be a link between the Third Reich and society's treatment of nonhuman animals is hard for most people to grasp. That nonhuman animals could suffer as horribly and pathetically as humans in being reduced to industrialized products and industrial waste and treated with complete contempt—a clear link between Nazism and factory farming—contradicts thousands of years of teaching that humans are superior to animals in all respects. Not only is this a "humans versus animals" issue in the minds of most, but by this time the Holocaust has become iconic and "historical," whereas the human manufacture of animal suffering is so pervasive that many people find it hard even to regard the slaughter of animals as a form of violence. Yet there are those who believe, as I do, that the Holocaust and humankind's treatment of nonhuman animals can be reasonably and enlighteningly compared, and that the sufferings of the victims in both cases can also be reasonably and enlighteningly compared. Allow me to say something about my own experience in this regard.

When I was in college in the 1960s, the three most important events in my life at the time were the German concentration camps, Stalin's slave labor camps, and the Civil Rights Movement. Growing up in the railroad town of Altoona, Pennsylvania in the 1940s and '50s, I saw suffering on a personal level. As well, the hushed tones and incensed voices of my parents and their friends discussing events overseas filtered into my consciousness. I was born during World War Two, and the War and its aftermath, including the polio epidemic of the 1950s, affected the atmosphere of our home and neighborhood. If today the discussion revolves around George W. Bush, the Middle East, Terrorism, Oil, AIDS, and Global Warming, back then it was the Iron Curtain, the Iron Lung, Hitler, Stalin, Communism, and the Atom Bomb. Along with the anxiety these words produced, this nomenclature was a significant part of the world in which I grew up. But it wasn't until I went to college that I began to understand once and for all the enormity of human suffering in the world.

In college I became active in the racial conflicts that were just then beginning to surface on campus, paralleling the growth of the Civil Rights Movement on the national level. At the same time, I plunged into books about Hitler and Stalin in my history classes, fatally attracted to the horrors these men had brought forth. So immersed did I become in the concentration camps and the slave labor camps, imagining what it must have felt like to be in one of those places, and the mentality that produced them—a mentality that was remarkably similar to the racial attitudes in America during that time— that I had to leave school. One autumn day, my father visited me and we talked about my going to law school to become a civil rights lawyer. Two weeks later, I called my parents to come and get me. I dropped out of college, unable to cope with my growing obsession with the human-engineered suffering of people that was like a cancer eating me alive, a movie reel that wound and rewound in insidious permutations, and still carry on as a student.

I was never in a concentration camp, and I do not pretend to equate my experience with the experience of those who were. Yet the fact remains that learning about the camps affected my adult perspective at the threshold more profoundly than any other single event up to that time. My subsequent preoccupation with the suffering of billions of nonhuman animals, far from being an abandonment of the perceptions I gained in the course of my preoccupation with the concentration camps and the Civil Rights Movement in the 1960s, involved a radical extension of those perceptions to include the largest class of innocent victims on earth.

I mention my college experience because in this book I argue that one group's experience with suffering is unique, but not in such a way that it precludes comparison with the suffering of other groups. An experience of oppression, such as the Holocaust, may serve as an appropriate metaphor to reveal similarities inherent in other forms of oppression, such as the oppression of nonhuman animals by human beings.

Use of Metaphor to Illuminate Atrocity

A metaphor is a figure of speech in which a word or phrase denoting one kind of object, action, or experience is used in place of another to suggest a likeness between them. A purpose of metaphor is to provide a familiar language and imagery to characterize new perceptions. In the case of atrocity, a key purpose of these perceptions is to generate concern and inspire action on behalf of the victims. When the oppression of one group is used metaphorically to illuminate the oppression of another group, justice requires that the oppression that forms the basis of the comparison be comprehended in its own right. The originating oppression that generates the metaphor must not be treated as a mere figure of speech, a mere point of reference. It must not be treated illogically as a lesser matter than that which it is being used to draw attention to.

However, if these requirements have been met, there is no good reason to insist that one form of suffering and oppression is so exclusive that it may not be used to raise moral concerns about any other form of oppression. A perfect match of oppressions or calculus of which group suffered more isn't necessary to make reasonable comparisons between them. If a person is offended by the comparisons regardless, it may be that the resentment is more proprietary than just and thereby represents an arbitrary delimiting of moral boundaries.

Even so, resentment can come from the sense that the uniqueness of one's own group experience with suffering is being appropriated to fit the experience of another group. For the victims of an atrocity such as the Holocaust, to be reduced to a mere point of reference is intolerable. The people involved have already endured having their individuality effaced and their identities diminished. Holocaust victims were forced to become instruments and objects in the service of their own extermination. The very presumption of putting their experience into words, particularly by one who "wasn't there," is impertinent, although eliminating the experience from the language, from memory, however inadequately preserved, must surely be worse.

A problem that remains to be solved, notwithstanding, is how to win attention to sufferers and suffering that most people do not want to hear about, or have trouble imagining, or would just as soon forget. One way is to use an analogy (a logical parallel), or a metaphor (a suggested likeness) that already has meaning and resonance in the public mind. For example, oppressed people, such as slaughterhouse workers or people who raise chickens for the poultry industry, say of themselves, "We are treated like animals."

Matt Prescott, the creator of the controversial "Holocaust on Your Plate" exhibit for People for the Ethical Treatment of Animals, argues that the analogy works both ways. His exhibit, which consists of eight 60-square-foot panels, each juxtaposing photographs of factory farms and slaughterhouses with photographs from Nazi death camps, depicts the point made by Yiddish writer and Nobel laureate Isaac Bashevis Singer, who in his short story "The Letter Writer" wrote, "In relation to [animals], all people are Nazis" (Singer 1982, 271). Prescott, who is himself a Jew with relatives who died under the Nazis, says that "when Holocaust survivors today try to relate the horrors they lived through, this is the very first analogy that comes to mind. They say, 'we were treated like animals'" (Prescott, 2003b).

Just as the animal analogy springs readily to mind to convey a spectrum of injustices perpetrated by people against one another, so in contemporary political discourse does the

Holocaust. So handy a metaphor for injustice, real or imaginary, has the Holocaust become that the president of Americans for Tax Reform, Grover Norquist, in an interview with Terry Gross on the National Public Radio program *Fresh Air*, compared rich Americans threatened with higher taxes to victims of the Holocaust. Norquist said:

> The morality that says it's okay to do something to a group because they're a small percentage of the population is the morality that says that the Holocaust is okay because they didn't target everybody, just a small percentage. . . . Arguing that it's okay to loot some group because it's them, and because it's a small number—that has no place in a democratic society (Lapham, 11).

On a more apposite note, in 1993, Congress and President Clinton authorized the construction of a national memorial museum to honor the victims of communism. The act cited "the deaths of over 100,000,000 victims in an unprecedented imperial communist holocaust" and resolved that "the sacrifices of these victims should be permanently memorialized so that never again will nations and peoples allow so evil a tyranny to terrorize the world" (Rauch, 28).

Clearly, a problem of definition arises when hundreds of "holocausts" permeate the language, when every act of violence, from rape to firing squads, constitutes a "holocaust." As Roberta Kalechofsky writes in *Animal Suffering and the Holocaust: The Problem with Comparisons*, when every atrocity becomes a holocaust, "each victim, human or animal, Jew or non-Jew, becomes a generalized metaphor for any other victim, and understanding of the how and the why of cruel institutions such as slavery or war or concentration camps is obliterated. History is obliterated in a wash of metaphors" (34). Similarly, historian Peter Pulzer has observed that when every expulsion from a village is genocide, "we no longer know how to recognize genocide. When Auschwitz is everywhere, it is nowhere" (Klug, 29).

Notwithstanding, the history of the twentieth century makes the "everywhereness of Auschwitz" seem not so far-fetched. It was "a century that had spawned two world wars, totalitarianism, genocide, concentration camps and nuclear warfare," the writer A. Alvarez notes in his memoir (189). Historian Enzo Traverso writes in his book *The Origins of Nazi Violence*:

> The brute violence of the SS special units (*Einsatzgruppen*) was not a feature peculiar to National Socialism. Rather, it was an indication of how much National Socialism had in common with plenty of other lethal ideologies of the terrible twentieth century that condoned massacres, ranging from the mass executions of Armenians in the Ottoman Empire to the ethnic cleansing operations in the former Yugoslavia and the machete slaughtering in Rwanda (14).

But, Traverso claims, there is a difference:

> Unlike these, however, the Jewish genocide constituted not only an eruption of brute violence but also a killing operation perpetrated "without hatred," thanks to a planned system designed for the production of death on an industrial scale, a mechanical apparatus created by a minority of architects of crime and operated by a mass of executioners—some of them zealous, the rest unthinking—amid the silent indifference of the greater majority of the German population and with the complicity of Europe and a passive world. Therein lies the singularity of the Jewish genocide (14).

However, for some, perhaps many, it is the "singularity" of the Jewish genocide—the formation by a cadre of individuals of a vast industrial killing operation conducted "without hatred" for the victims amid the silent indifference and complicity of a passive world—that evokes comparisons with the modern industrialized systems of exploiting animals. As Matt Prescott writes, "Comparisons to the Holocaust are undeniable and inescapable not only because we humans share with all other animals our ability to feel pain, fear and loneliness, but because the government-sanctioned oppression of billions of beings, and the systems we use to abuse and kill them, eerily parallel the concentration camps" (2003b). He explains:

> The methods of the Holocaust exist today in the form of factory farming where billions of innocent, feeling beings are taken from their families, trucked hundreds of miles through all weather extremes, confined in cramped, filthy conditions, and herded to their deaths. During the Holocaust, hundreds of thousands of men, women and children died from heat exhaustion, dehydration, starvation, or from freezing to the sides of cattle cars. Those who arrived at the concentration camps alive were forced into cramped bunkers where they lived on top of other dead victims, covered in their own feces and urine. They were forced to work until their bodies couldn't work anymore, and were then herded to their deaths in assembly-line fashion.
>
> Ten billion animals a year in the US suffer through these same horrors every single day. We must ask ourselves: sixty years later, have we learned nothing? Why are we still transporting animals through all weather extremes, forcing them to endure extreme heat and cold? Why are we still confining them in conditions so dirty,

the only way to keep them alive is through the extreme overuse of antibiotics? Why are we still ripping children away from mothers and leading them by the necks and legs to the kill floor? (Prescott, 2003b)

A former pharmaceutical company employee with the poultry industry, JoAnn Farb, wrote afterward:

[O]ne of my worst experiences, and it didn't even involve live animals, was the World Poultry Expo in Atlanta. It horrified me because its energy and unquestioned acceptance paralleled a holocaust concentration camp. I would walk through the aisles and think, 'I am probably one of the few people here (out of thousands) who find this disturbing'—and I found that very disturbing (letter quoted in Davis 1996, 19).

An engineer wrote in the *Baltimore Sun*, "About 20 years ago, *Scientific American* ran an article on the management of chickens in the production of eggs and meat. Concentration camps for chickens is what one friend who read the article called the chicken farms" (Burruss).

One may counter that while there have been thousands of concentration camps erected for various purposes, there was only one Holocaust. The camps have a longer history and a wider frame of reference than the Jewish experience under the Nazis, even though that experience arose out of centuries of organized and spontaneous oppression of the Jewish people under various empires. The concentration camps that proliferated during World War One grew out of the internment by the British of the Boers, South African civilians whose ancestors were Dutch colonists, during the Boer War of 1899–1902. Before that, "the first modern concentration camps" appeared in Cuba, when imperial Spain forced insurgent Cuban peasants off their land and stuck them in camps (Applebaum, xxxiv). From there concentration camps multiplied during World War One in Europe, India, Japan, Australia, Canada, and Africa. First set up as temporary compounds for displaced civilian populations and prisoners of war, these camps became fixed institutions, and it was during this time, Enzo Traverso explains, between 1914 and 1918, that "the expression 'concentration camps' entered the vocabulary of Western countries" (86).

II.
Etymology of the Word "Holocaust"

In their first applications to unnamed events, terms like "holocaust," "sho'ah," or "churban" necessarily evoked other destructions in order to frame the catastrophe of European Jewry during World War II. Unlike English or Armenian cultural lexicons, however, Jewish tradition already contained not only a set of possible precedents and terms like churban *or* sho'ah *by which to know the latest destruction, but also ritual days of lament, during which all catastrophes—past, present, and future—are recalled at once. Whether or not the Bar Kochba rebellion, and the massacre of Europe's Jews are equivalent events, upon sharing the same name, each event is automatically grasped in light of its namesake.*—James E. Young, *Writing and Rewriting the Holocaust*

In an ironic but significant twist to the cataloguing of historical periods, the massacre of nearly one and a half million Armenians by the Turks between 1915 and 1923 has come recently to be known as the "Armenian Holocaust": it is ironic in that the Armenian massacre has been made to rely for its name on a set of events that postdate it by twenty-five years, and significant in that it is now thus figured for Armenians in the terms of another people's catastrophe.—**James E. Young**, *Writing and Rewriting the Holocaust*

When, and by what route, did the word "holocaust" enter the vocabulary of Western countries? In his essay "The Holocaust—One Generation Later," Nazi concentration camp analyst Bruno Bettelheim bristles that "it was not the hapless victims of the Nazis who named their incomprehensible and totally unmasterable fate the 'holocaust.' It was the Americans who applied this artificial and highly technical term to the Nazi extermination of the European Jews" (91). "Holocaust," Bettelheim argues, is a "linguistic circumlocution" designed to protect us from the raw facts that, expressed in meaningful language, would overwhelm us with "catastrophe beyond comprehension, beyond the limits of our imagination, unless we force ourselves against our desire to extend it to encompass these terrible events" (91). The true holocausts, Bettelheim argues, were sacred Hebrew rituals:

The correct definition of "holocaust" is "burnt offering." As such, it is part of the language of the psalmist, a meaningful word to all who have some acquaintance with the Bible, full of the richest emotional connotations. By using the term "holocaust," entirely false associations are established through conscious and unconscious connotations between the most vicious of mass murders and ancient rituals of a deeply religious nature.

Using a word with such strong unconscious religious connotations when speaking of the murder of millions of Jews robs the victims of this abominable mass murder of the only thing left to them: their uniqueness. Calling the most callous, most brutal, most horrid, most heinous mass murder a burnt offering is a sacrilege, a profanation of God and man (92).

In reality, however, the word holocaust is neither species-specific nor culture-specific. The term was taken over from the Greek word *holokauston*, which in ancient times denoted their own and others' cultural practice of sacrificing animals, to designate the Nazi extermination of the European Jews. Conceivably, those animals could complain that their experience of being forcibly turned into burnt offerings (and to please or sate a god they would not necessarily have acknowledged as their god) has been unjustly appropriated by their victimizers, who are robbing them of *their* original experience of suffering. Taking the animals' view, it may be said of them, as Bettelheim said of the millions of Jews and others who were systematically slaughtered by the Nazis, that "while these millions were slaughtered for an idea, they did not die for one" (93).

In *Animals in the Third Reich: Pets, Scapegoats, and the Holocaust*, Boria Sax writes that the "very word *Holocaust* pertains to animal sacrifice" (156). Sax explains that among the people of the ancient Mediterranean, the slaughter of animals was generally "a festive occasion with the inedible parts, bones, and gall bladder together with a little meat left on the altar for a deity, while the rest was consumed by human beings" (156).

In Hebrew sacrifice, a Holocaust was the entire animal "given to Yahweh to be consumed by fire. The prototype was the sacrifice of the shepherd Abel to Yahweh from his flock." Use of the word holocaust for the Nazi murders, according to Sax, is "based on an identification between the Jewish people and the sacrificed animal. The imagery parallels the way Christ is traditionally represented as the sacrificial lamb. In a strange way the term *Holocaust* equates the Nazis, as those who perform the sacrifice, with priests of ancient Israel" (156).

Likewise, in his discussion of the etymology of the word holocaust, Jon Petrie shows that the word did not suddenly "jump out of the Bible" into the English language, nor was its original meaning limited to Hebrew religious sacrifice or to Judeo-Christian offerings. Before it entered the Septuagint, the Greek translation of the Hebrew Bible, the word holocaust "denoted pagan sacrifices," including "a pagan sacrifice to a false god" (Petrie, 3). Contrary to scholarly assertions that the word holocaust carries deep religious Judeo-Christian connotations to English-speaking people via the Bible, Petrie notes that the term "holocaust" does not even appear in the King James Bible and that the Hebrew term *olah*, translated by Greek scholars as "burnt offerings" (*holokauston*) has not been translated as "holocaust" in a Protestant Bible since c. 1600. Nor has the word *olah* ever been translated as "holocaust" in a Jewish Bible (2).

Petrie disputes efforts to invest the word holocaust with pure honorific scriptural significance and to limit its modern use to the Nazi genocide of the Jews. He shows that the word was in broad secular use before the 1940s and '50s—the period when the word holocaust, "in addition to its use as a referent to a wide variety of other events," began to appear occasionally as "a referent to the mass murder of Jews in the Hitler period or to both the mass murder and preceding persecutions" (3).

For writers and editors of the pre-1950 *Palestine Post*, Petrie points out that "holocaust" had a "broad range of possible referents" and did not carry "deep religious, Judeo-Christian connotations" (3). Examples from the *Palestine Post* of 1938 show that the word holocaust was used to denote: a replacement of German officials by others ("the bloodless holocaust of German Generals and Ambassadors"); Japanese raids against China ("Japanese aeroplanes again raided Canton. Although the damage exceeds September's holocaust, the death toll was somewhat less"); World War I ("that holocaust swept over the world" and "the general dread of yet another European holocaust"); and Bolshevist purges ("The holocaust of directors and engineers shot as 'wreckers'"). A 1940 *Palestine Post* advertisement for "Mandrake the Magician" promises "a flaming holocaust of thrills," and a column on July 26, 1946 calls housecleaning that consists of "crashing china and glasses" a "holocaust of housework." As late as May 9, 1947, the *Palestine Post* called the May 4, 1897 explosion of a cinema projector lightbulb in a tent filled with 1,200 people, a "holocaust, which lasted 20 brief minutes" and "claimed 124 lives" (Petrie, 2–3).

Although the word holocaust is used in the Israeli Declaration of Independence on May 15, 1948 in reference to the Jewish genocide under Hitler, and in scattered other places, the Israeli English use of the word as a referent for the Nazi extermination of the Jewish people did not spread in the United States until the early 1960s. Political and social philosopher Hannah Arendt's series of articles in *The New Yorker* in 1963, which covered the trial of German Nazi leader Adolf Eichmann and was published that same year as *Eichmann in Jerusalem: A Report on the Banality of Evil*, helped to disseminate the term thus defined as well as to encourage greater interest in the Nazi murders at a time when the most common referent of "holocaust" was nuclear war and destruction. For example, the November 4, 1961 cover of *The Nation* announces: "SHELTERS WHEN THE HOLOCAUST COMES" (Petrie, 4).

Petrie thinks that American Jewish writers "probably abandoned such words as 'disaster,' 'catastrophe,' and 'massacre' in favor of 'holocaust' in the 1960s" because "holocaust" with its evocation of the then dreaded annihilation effectively conveyed something of the horror of the Jewish experience during World War Two. Increasingly, in the 1970s, holocaust was capitalized and consigned to that singular use, although from the 1980s to the present the word has sometimes been expanded to include the Nazi persecution and murder of both Jewish and non-Jewish people. This expansion has caused consternation among those Jews who feel, for example, that "broadening the meaning of the word Holocaust to encompass murder of segments of other population groups is a vicious attempt to diminish the rights of the Jewish survivors of this horror to point the finger at the perpetrators" (Petrie, 1).

Yet there is precedent for contextualizing the word more broadly. The United States Holocaust Museum states in its guidelines for teaching about the Holocaust that "The Holocaust provides a context for exploring the dangers of remaining silent, apathetic, and indifferent in the face of others' oppression." Holocaust survivors themselves broaden the word contextually when they say, "we were treated like animals." As Matt Prescott tells those who protest when the analogy is reversed: "Holocaust victims WERE treated like animals, and so logically we can conclude that animals are treated like Holocaust victims" (2004).

As with most things, the Holocaust obtained its current identity gradually, over time. That identity grew in fits and starts, from ancient beginnings denoting pagan and Hebrew sacrifice, to modern secular usages. Notably, the word's origin attracts almost no attention; in particular, one seldom or never thinks about the animal victims of ancient and modern holocaust rituals. Although I studied the Bible as required by the Presbyterian college I attended as a freshman, the many references to animal sacrifice in Exodus and Leviticus never registered on my consciousness. Not until I was asked by *Best Friends* magazine, in 2003, to express an opinion on whether the PETA "Holocaust on Your Plate" exhibit "went too far" (Munro) did Bruno Bettelheim's definition of "holocaust" as a "burnt offering" with deep religious significance spring to mind.

And while many Jews resent the use of the word "holocaust" to characterize other forms of atrocity, we see that

American Jewish writers in the 1960s sought to express and draw attention to the Jewish experience under the Nazis by invoking the "holocaust" of nuclear war to achieve this goal. Furthermore, Holocaust survivors and their descendents regularly invoke "animals" to characterize the Jewish nightmare under Hitler. Nor is this usage universally resented when the analogy is reversed. As noted, Nobel laureate Isaac Bashevis Singer (1904–91), who grew up in a Polish village where his father was a Hasidic rabbi, has one of his fictional characters, Herman Gombiner, say in the short story "The Letter Writer" that towards the animals, all humans are Nazis, and for the animals, every day is Treblinka. (Treblinka was a Nazi death camp in Poland that began operating in 1942.) Herman, who lost his entire family to the Nazis, is thinking about a mouse he befriended whose death he believes he caused, and his sadness leads to a larger thought:

> In his thoughts, Herman spoke a eulogy to the mouse who had shared a portion of her life with him and who, because of him, had left this earth. "What do they know—all those scholars, all those philosophers, all the leaders of the world—about such as you? They have convinced themselves that man, the worst transgressor of all the species, is the crown of creation. All other creatures were created merely to provide him with food, pelts, to be tormented, exterminated. In relation to them, all people are Nazis; for the animals it is an eternal Treblinka. And yet man demands compassion from heaven" (Singer 1982, 271).

Herman's sentiment, which is a principle theme throughout Singer's work, has been and continues to be echoed by many Jewish people, many of whom are pioneers, leaders, and activists in the modern animal rights movement. Their views are represented, and many of them are vividly profiled, in Holocaust historian Charles Patterson's book *Eternal Treblinka: Our Treatment of Animals and the Holocaust*. In *Eternal Treblinka*, Patterson explores the many parallels between our treatment of nonhuman animals and our treatment of humans considered to be less than human. Patterson writes, for example, regarding the age-old use of animals to denigrate other people:

> The great divide between humans and animals provided a standard by which to judge other people, both at home and elsewhere. If the essence of humanity was defined as consisting of a specific quality or set of qualities, such as reason, intelligible language, religion, culture, or manners, it followed that anyone who did not fully possess those qualities was "subhuman." Those judged less than human were seen either as useful beasts to be curbed, domesticated, and kept docile, or as predators or vermin to be eliminated.
>
> This hierarchical thinking, built on the enslavement/domestication of animals that began 11,000 years ago, condoned and encouraged the oppression of people regarded as animals or animal-like. The ethic of human domination which promotes and justifies the exploitation of animals legitimized the oppression of humans alleged to be in an animal condition. The German biologist and philosopher Ernst Haeckel (1834–1919), whose ideas had a strong influence on Nazi ideology, maintained that since non-European races are "psychologically nearer to the mammals (apes and dogs) than to civilized Europeans, we must, therefore, *assign a totally different value to their lives*" (Patterson, 25–26).

To summarize, the Holocaust assumed its present signification through an accumulation of contexts. Through a history of associations, the holocaust as an image of human-manufactured horror was already in place when it finally came to denote, in the 1960s, the Jewish genocide under the Nazis. And the term was needed, for as Michael Lerner writes in *Healing Israel/Palestine*, in the 1960s, not only the rest of the world but even liberal and progressive movements that spoke on behalf of other minority groups "were woefully inadequate in speaking to the situation of the Jewish people just a few decades after the genocide of Jews in the 1940s" (13).

Based on the above it seems fair to contend that an over-whelming oppression may legitimately be used to illuminate other overwhelming oppressions, bearing in mind the limitations of comparative analysis in this as in any other area. After all, no two oppressions are exactly alike. Even the psychologies of hate, humiliation, and cruelty break down to subtler distinctions, as do the institutions that reflect and perpetuate them. To compare two institutions of cruelty, such as the prisons and workhouses of the nineteenth century with the concentration camps of the twentieth century, is not, as Enzo Traverso has pointed out, to equate them. Yet even if their origins and final aims were different, he writes, there are elements in these institutions that were substantially similar: "the confined place, the coerced labor, the 'useless violence,' the military type of discipline, the punishments, the total absence of liberty, the uniform, the exhaustion of bodies, the inhumane living conditions, and the humiliation" (Traverso, 32).

This approach bolsters my contention that an atrocity such as the Holocaust may serve as a strategic metaphor to illuminate and promote action on behalf of other innocent victims, including the oppression of nonhuman animals by human beings. Obviously there are risks that the compared atrocities could lose their identities and become mere interchangeable, rhetorical tropes, ironically subverting the very purpose of making the comparisons in the first place. But care to prevent this outcome is not a prima facie reason to cancel the project because there are dangers in it. An incommensurable oppression may retain its identity while shedding light on other immeasurable magnitudes of suffering and injustice in the world. It may, as Susan Sontag says of the art of depicting atrocity in her book *Regarding the Pain of Others*, disclose "new subjects for fellow feeling" and be "a turning point in the history of moral feelings and of sorrow—as deep, as original, as demanding" (Sontag, 44–45).

Chapter Two

EVIDENCE OF THINGS NOT SEEN

It began with one pig at a British slaughterhouse. Somewhere along the production line it was observed that the animal had blisters in his mouth and was salivating. The worst suspicions were confirmed, and within days borders had been sealed and a course of action determined. Soon all of England and the world watched as hundreds, and then hundreds of thousands, of pigs, cows, and sheep and their newborn lambs were taken outdoors, shot, thrown into burning pyres, and bulldozed into muddy graves. Reports described terrified cattle being chased by sharpshooters, clambering over one another to escape. Some were still stirring and blinking a day after being shot. . . . These animals, millions of them not even infected, were all killed only because their market value had been diminished and because trade policies required it— because, in short, under the circumstances it was the quick and convenient thing to do. By the one measure we now apply to these creatures, they had all become worthless. For them, the difference between what happened and what awaited them anyway was one of timing. And for us the difference was visibility. This time, we had to watch.—**Matthew Scully** on the extermination of animals in the foot-and-mouth disease epidemic of 2001, *Dominion: The Power of Man, the Suffering of Animals, and the Call to Mercy*

21

The killing and disposal of nine million hens is gallocide on a scale too vast for the average imagination. . . . [P]erhaps the destruction in our age of millions of human beings who were thought to carry a kind of racial virus in their genes has inured us to the horror of killing so many living creatures and left us equally indifferent to the strange developments which make such a solution seem inevitable if not commonplace.
—**Page Smith and Charles Daniel**, *The Chicken Book*, on the extermination of chickens in southern California in the 1970s to combat Newcastle disease and raise the price of eggs

As I begin writing this chapter in the spring of 2004, a global massacre of animals is being conducted and reported by the news media. Millions of chickens, turkeys, and ducks are being gassed, clubbed to death, buried alive, and burned alive, on television and in the newspapers. Villagers in Bali, Indonesia are burning up thousands of chickens to get rid of the "evil spirits" on which they blame the current disease outbreak of influenza that rages periodically and festers continuously in poultry flocks living in conditions of mass concentration and human-perpetrated filth (AP, Feb. 11, 2004). In just one day, 118,000 six-week-old chickens were exterminated on a single farm in Maryland (MDA). In Southeast Asia, to contain a virulent strain of the H5N1 avian influenza that can infect and kill people as well as birds, 80 million chickens were exterminated between late January and mid-February (Henderson). In Canada, 19 million birds were exterminated to control the disease (Muhtadie).

It's been said that if most people had direct contact with the animals they consume, vegetarianism would soar, but history has yet to support this hope. It wasn't only the Nazis who could see birds in the yard, slaughter them, and eat them without a qualm, and in fact with euphoria. Whether consciously

cruel, morally indifferent, or afflicted with what former vivi-
sector turned animal rights activist Donald Barnes called "conditioned ethical blindness" (Barnes 162), most people do not
want to see the animals they consume and are remarkably able
to avoid seeing them, even when the victims are looking right
back at them in, for instance, a live poultry market (UPC
2004b). In many parts of the world today, animals are driven,
as they have been for millennia, to market on foot. They are
tied up and crated among the vegetables and killed out in the
open, and people do not object.

Isaac Bashevis Singer describes vividly in his writings the
slaughter of animals that he witnessed in the courtyards of the
Polish villages he grew up in. In the short story "The
Slaughterer," Singer draws upon his experience to how, in public view, "the butchers chopped the cows with their axes and
skinned them before they had heaved their last breath. The
women plucked the feathers from chickens while they were
still alive" (Singer 1982, 209). When the main character,
Yoineh Meir, is appointed by the rabbi to become the town's
ritual slaughterer, Meir's hatred of his work and his vicarious
suffering with the animals he kills alienates him from the community. What for him is torture is for other people a festive
occasion:

> A week before the New Year, there was a rush of slaugh-
> tering. All day long, Yoineh Meir stood near a pit,
> slaughtering hens, roosters, geese, ducks. Women
> pushed, argued, tried to get to the slaughterer first.
> Others joked, laughed, bantered. Feathers flew, the yard
> was full of quacking, gabbling, the screaming of roost-
> ers. Now and then a fowl cried out like a human being
> (Singer 1982, 213).

In modern industrial society, the transport and killing of

animals takes place mostly out of sight, though not for the people who do the work—yet how many workers identify with their victims, or become vegetarians? Virgil Butler, who worked in a Tyson chicken slaughterhouse for five years, said of the chickens, paralyzed with electric shocks before having their throats cut, "Their muscles don't work, but their eyes do and you can tell by them looking at you, they're scared to death" (Butler 2003).

Historian Enzo Traverso says that the Nazis created an industrial system for slaughter in which the victims were simply the "raw material" necessary for the "mass production of corpses" (45). An animal researcher tells meat producers that "slaughter is different from processing in that the raw material is alive, has a central nervous system, can express emotional states, and has biological components like humans" (Swanson). However, in his review of Jeffrey Masson's book *The Pig Who Sang to the Moon: The Emotional World of Farm Animals* (2003), B. R. Myers writes that research could prove "that cows love Jesus, and the line at the McDonald's drive-through wouldn't be one sagging carload shorter the next day" (Myers, 115). Only consider: in Salisbury, Maryland, a McDonald's sits on one side of the street and on the other side a gigantic chicken slaughter plant looms, surrounded by its endlessly sagging truckloads of chickens waiting on the dock to be killed. There is no clear evidence that the sight of suffering evokes sympathy or protest in the majority of people, and the first shock of seeing suffering can wear off. Even if it doesn't, people can choose not to look.

The fact that animals are suffering and dying for appetites that could be satisfied in many other ways makes some, perhaps many, people uncomfortable, though not necessarily because of guilt. People get annoyed that you're bothering them, trying to curtail their freedom and uncover a guilt that they may not feel, or don't feel strongly enough, so that some end up feeling "guilty" because they don't feel guilty, just vexed that they're being victimized. Myers calls this reaction a "cold-blooded squeamishness," like that of "the German villagers who scowled into their handkerchiefs rather than behold the corpses in liberated death camps." Try forcing most Americans to consider the suffering of the animals they consume, Myers says, and they will conclude, "like those German villagers, that the whole exercise has more to do with punishment than persuasion" (116–117).

Undramatic Suffering

Animal suffering, obviously, is not the only suffering that is ignored. As Susan Sontag articulates in *Regarding the Pain of Others*, getting people to pay attention to human suffering imposed by other people isn't easy. Wars of comparable magnitude and cruelty seldom receive comparable attention outside the locality in which they occur. For example, the Chaco War (1932–35), a butchery in Bolivia and Paraguay that killed 100,000 soldiers, was covered by a photojournalist "whose superb close-up battle pictures are as forgotten as that war" (Sontag 2003, 35–36). In *Gulag: A History*, Anne Applebaum quotes a reviewer of her book about the former Soviet Union who wrote: "Here occurred the terror famine of the 1930s, in which Stalin killed more Ukrainians than Hitler murdered Jews. Yet how many in the West remember it? After all, the killing was so—so boring, and ostensibly undramatic" (Applebaum, xix).

Seeking to explain the relative failure of the Soviet concentration camps to enter the popular consciousness of the West—the vast system of forced labor, mass murder, mass terror, and exile which lasted from 1918 until 1953, absorbed some 18 million people, and which prisoners called the "meat-grinder"—historian Pierre Rigoulot argues that not only the development of human knowledge, "but also its stagnation or retreat, depends on the social, cultural and political framework" (Applebaum, xviii). For a war or other atrocity to win the collective attention and claim the memory of non-victims, it must have larger ramifications and "uniqueness" than being merely local and routine. It has to have broad political and economic significance, similar to the way in which diseases that affect relatively few people, like SARS (Severe Acute Respiratory Syndrome), gain worldwide attention and funding where international trade is involved (Greger; MacKenzie, et al.), whereas diseases that affect many more people more cruelly for years, like AIDS in Africa, get little of either (Goodwin, 19).

Dramatic Suffering

A major prerequisite for winning the attention of a particular group of people to the plight of others consists in the ability of the victims and their advocates to create a compelling narrative drama in an interpretive framework that unites the history and identities of both groups. Whatever the Holocaust may mean to the majority of the world's people, in Western culture it has achieved an iconic status, not only because of the facts themselves but because of the primacy of the written word in Jewish history. In *Writing and Rewriting the Holocaust*, James E. Young places the Holocaust "survivor-scribe" within the Jewish tradition of narrative testimony in which the "lexicon of destruction" has been gathered in sacred and scholarly texts that are revered and claimed by both Jews and their Christian descendants. Young cites, for example, the effect of Hannah Arendt's entering the Eichmann trial in Jerusalem into the public record, arguing that through such authoritative writing, embedded in "the centuries of historical archetypes for suffering accumulated in Hebrew," the Holocaust became "part of a larger realm of experiences constituting language itself" (Young, 132–134).

This raises the question of how much comparable suffering

never enters the public mind or the history books simply because the sufferers did not, or could not, articulate their experience in terms of the requisite social, cultural and political framework in a narrative of compelling speech. Was the Holocaust really the worst atrocity in the history of the world? Why is the Holocaust more real to me than many other horrors, and is the same thing true for the entire human population? Was what the Nazis did to the Jews more deeply horrible, for example, than what the Europeans—whose creed was "exterminate or banish"—did to the Native Americans, as documented in *Bury My Heart at Wounded Knee: An Indian History of the American West* (Brown, 65) and elsewhere? Not according to Native American scholar Ward Churchill, who writes: "The American holocaust was and remains unparalleled, both in terms of its magnitude and the degree to which its goals were met, and in terms of the extent to which its ferocity was sustained over time by not one but several participating groups" (Churchill 1997, 4).

Conditions Favoring the Invisibility of Others

In his essay "Marrakech," George Orwell describes his experience in the Moroccan town of Marrakech in the 1930s, when Morocco was still under European colonial rule and Hitler was just coming to power. He describes contemplating people and their suffering under circumstances where watching people was "almost like watching a flock of cattle."

> When you walk through a town like this—two hundred thousand inhabitants, of whom at least twenty thousand own literally nothing except the rags they stand up in—when you see how the people live, and still more easily how they die, it is always difficult to believe that you are walking among human beings. All colonial empires are in reality founded upon that fact. The peo-

ple have brown faces—besides, there are so many of
them! Are they really the same flesh as yourself? Do
they even have names? Or are they merely a kind of
undifferentiated brown stuff, about as individual as bees
or coral insects? They rise out of the earth, they sweat
and starve for a few years, and then they sink back into
the nameless mounds of the graveyard and nobody
notices that they are gone. And even the graves themselves soon fade back into the soil. Sometimes, out for a
walk, as you break your way through the prickly pear,
you notice that it is rather bumpy under foot, and only
a certain regularity in the bumps tells you that you are
walking over skeletons.

Orwell's perspective is that of a middle-class Englishman
and member of the European ruling class, except that Orwell
seeks to understand the experience of not seeing others. One
wonders whether he is serious when he says that when these
people die, "nobody notices that they are gone." Who is
"nobody"? Is Orwell suggesting that the subjugated people of
Marrakech are as personally negligible to one another as they
are to him and the culture he represents? Even the cattle
Orwell cites for comparison—do they exist mainly in anonymous, "replaceable" relationships within their own societies?[1]

Orwell suggests through the image of the "great white birds
drifting like scraps of paper" overhead that the white masters of
Marrakech are ultimately as negligible in the overall scheme of
things as the people they rule are in their eyes. Yet this is not to
say that the rulers themselves don't suffer, or that their suffering doesn't matter, even in the face of an indifferent universe.
Could the same thing be said of the cattle, bees, and other animals who pass through the world unseen by most people?

II.
Historical vs Hidden Suffering

In *Animal Suffering and the Holocaust: The Problem with Comparisons*, Roberta Kalechofsky writes: "There is no proof that the flesh of a burning human being is hotter than the flesh of a burning animal. We may think so because the human race has left a record of its suffering, and the animals have not. They have lived their pain, in secret places, with little trace on human consciousness. The gifts of language and writing—in short, of history—have brought for us greater attention and consciousness of our suffering, while animal suffering is barely accorded knowledge. It is history which separates animal suffering from the Holocaust" (Kalechofsky, 34–35).

Yes, and it is "history" that separates from the Holocaust not only animal suffering but also the millennia of unrecorded human suffering, including the unrecorded human victims of the Nazis. None of us knows, omnisciently, who suffers more in conditions of horror, human or nonhuman individuals. It may be that beyond a certain point, we cannot fully apprehend the reality of anyone else's suffering. In her book *The Body in Pain*, Elaine Scarry says that "A person whose pain it is, knows it effortlessly, the person whose pain it is not, cannot know it even with effort" (Adams 1996, 183). While Scarry's subject is human pain and the inability of other people to fathom it, what she says applies to nonhuman animal suffering as well: "It is easy to remain wholly unaware of its existence; even with effort, one may remain in doubt about its existence or may retain the astonishing freedom of denying its existence; and finally, if with the best effort of sustained attention one successfully apprehends it, the aversiveness of the 'it' one apprehends will only be a shadowy fraction of the actual 'it'" (Adams 1996, 183).

The problem of apprehending the pain of others is increased when the others are in a situation of mass suffering. From the standpoint of onlookers, the individual is submerged in a sea of suffering. This is the opposite of the personal experience of being inside one's private hell while engulfed by the hell of others. No wonder people who have suffered as whole populations are desperate to be *seen*. No wonder they resent having their suffering compared to the suffering of another group. What is felt to be even worse than being "twinned" with another group is to be indistinguishable to all forms of consciousness outside one's own consciousness, which will be obliterated in one's own death.[2]

A fundamental difficulty in drawing attention to the plight of factory-farmed animals is, similarly, that every situation in which they appear is a mass situation, one that appears to be, as in reality it is, a limitless expanse of animal suffering and horror (Davis, 2004a). Every factory-farm scene replicates this expanse, mirroring its magnitude of unmanageability. Except for the "veal" calf, whose solitary confinement stall and large sad eyes draw attention to him- or herself as a desolate individual, all that most people see in looking at animal factories are endless rows of battery-caged hens, wall-to-wall turkeys, thousands of chickens or pigs. What they hear is deathly silence or indistinguishable "noise." They see a sepia sea of bodies without conflict, plot, or endpoint.

To the public eye, the sheer number and expanse of animals surrounded by metal, wires, dung, dander, and dust renders all of them invisible and impersonal. There are no "individuals," no drama on which to focus, only a scene of abstract suffering. Their pain is not even minimally grasped by most viewers, who are socialized not to perceive animals, especially "food" animals, as individuals with feelings. These onlookers have no concept of animals as sentient beings, let alone as individuals with projects of their own of which they have been stripped, such as their own family life and the comfort it brings, which was their birthright in nature.[3]

In *The Pig Who Sang to the Moon*, Jeffrey Masson shows how hard it is even for a sensitive person such as himself to apprehend the suffering of animals when thousands of them are crammed inside a building. Entering a gigantic shed filled with "broiler" chickens who are being raised for slaughter, Masson writes that on opening the door, "I was almost blinded by the sight of 25,000 pure white chickens, packed up right against one another as far as my eyes could see. It was like a hall of mirrors, never-ending chickens, all the same size, lined up one next to the other, eating the food, drinking the water, in artificial light, and in almost total silence" (Masson, 92).

Like Orwell looking at the "invisible" people of Marrakech, Masson sees these birds under circumstances that reflect their condition of mass subjugation, a condition more likely to obscure suffering than to reveal it. Seeing animals in industrialized settings such as factory farms encourages the view that animals are inherently passive objects whose only role in life is to serve the human enterprise. The role of the animal is to fit into human categories of sacrifice, science, and so forth. The term "scientific study" is ironic, for as philosopher Barbara Noske says regarding the place of animals in anthropology, "Far from being considered agents or subjects in their own right, the animals themselves are virtually overlooked" (Noske 1993, 1).

A glaring example of such oversight can be seen in studies of the human/nonhuman interaction known as "bestiality"— a term used to designate human sexual relations with/assault upon nonhuman animals. Historically, bestiality has entailed criminal prosecution and condemnation to death of both or all parties involved (Exodus 22: 19; Evans, 147–153; Beirne,

320–324; Davis 2001a, 89). In his article "Rethinking Bestiality: Towards a Concept of Interspecies Sexual Assault," criminology scholar Piers Beirne, of the University of Southern Maine, describes the anthropocentric neglect of the nonhuman animal victims from past to present:

> Seldom, either in times past or now, do popular images of social control include recognition of the terror and the pain that judicial interrogation and execution inflict on animals convicted of sexual relations with humans. Neither in the Mosaic commandments nor in the records of past or present court proceedings, neither in the rantings of puritan zealots nor in psychiatric testimony, is bestiality censured because of the harm that it inflicts on animals. But, especially in the case of smaller creatures like rabbits and hens, animals often suffer great pain and even death from human-animal sexual relations. While researchers have examined the physiological consequences of bestiality for humans (e.g., Tournier et al., 1981), they pay no attention to the internal bleeding, the ruptured anal passages, the bruised vaginas and the battered cloaca of animals, let alone to animals' psychological and emotional trauma. Such neglect of animal suffering mirrors the broader problem that, even when commentators admit the discursive relevance of animal abuse to the understanding of human societies, they do not perceive it, either theoretically or practically, as an object of study in its own right (Beirne, 324).

Ecology of Pain and Suffering

If animals are overlooked in the range of human endeavors based on their exploitation, is it any wonder that the suffering of animals is barely accorded human knowledge, and that it makes sense to speak of the "secret" and "hidden" suffering of animals? Even so, many people regard suffering in and of itself as morally objectionable. As the Reverend Dr. Humphry Primatt wrote in 1776, "Pain is Pain, whether it be inflicted on man or on beast; and the creature that suffers it, whether man or beast, being sensible of the misery of it whilst it lasts, suffers Evil" (Ryder, 66).

Yet the idea that pain and suffering are evil, simply because they *are* pain and suffering, is not always true (Davis 1989). Pain that is degrading in one situation may be uplifting in another, as when a person voluntarily suffers for the sake of a loved one or a worthwhile cause. Pain may be constructive as well as debilitating. In "A Critique of the Kantian Theory of Indirect Duties to Animals," Jeff Sebo writes, for example, that "people often claim that traumatic events serve as *catalysts* for rational behavior, helping them to reprioritize their lives and focus on what is important" (12). Some philosophers, Sebo writes, even claim that pain and suffering are important channels for rational development: "Aristotle, for example, argues that trauma is a cathartic experience that allows us to overcome emotive impulses in the future, while Nietzsche argues that masters of morality flourish in life only by overcoming severe physical and psychological challenges" (Sebo, 12).

At the most basic level, biologists remind us that pain is informative. Physical pain lets us know that we are injured or ill, just as, in the moral realm, guilt informs us that we have done wrong. Few would argue that a morally pain-free psychopath "isn't suffering" simply because the lack of a conscience is soothing to that person, and freedom from moral restraint is euphoric.

The fact is, not all pain is the same. While it is true that pain is pain regardless of who suffers it, other considerations apply. For instance, if I had to choose between suffering from cancer and suffering in a concentration camp, I would choose cancer.

Why? Because horrible as it is, cancer is not a sign of human character. It is a malignant physical disease, not a malignant assertion of human will. Cancer is unfortunate, whereas a concentration camp is evil. The fact that much human cancer today can be traced to products produced in chemical and industrial laboratories, and that corporate producers are notoriously resistant to remedying the harmful effects of their products, complicates but does not invalidate this distinction.

The contrast between human agency and random occurrence is important to counter the idea that it makes no difference whether a human or nonhuman animal, say, starves to death from natural causes or as part of someone's research; whether he suffers in the course of natural predation or in the machinery of somebody's factory farm or slave labor camp. Pain does not occur in a vacuum. Pain has a context. There are not only degrees and durations of pain; there are also causes and conditions, there may be motives and attitudes, that enter into it. Clearly seen, each episode of pain reflects the environment that produced it. Photographs of animals undergoing vivisection, Auschwitz inmates recounting their experience of being experimented on by Nazi doctors in the Nazis' "medical" milieu, the testimony of the doctors themselves (Lifton) show that there is a moral ecology of pain as well as a natural ecology of misfortune, which may or may not overlap.

Pain is a *symbol* in the sense of something that is a part of— that stands out from and illuminates—a larger reality. To talk meaningfully about pain, we must take into account the conditions under which it occurs, including the question of whether these conditions are primarily moral—involving human attitudes, motives, and conduct—or natural, like a plague or an earthquake. We will not then be confounded when someone dares to assert, as I once heard a researcher do at the National Institutes of Health concerning the head-bashing experiments that were then being conducted on baboons at the University of Pennsylvania, that what "happens" to animals in laboratories isn't so terrible, because "life is full of suffering."

Difference between Pain and Suffering

But are pain and suffering identical? Think of the question in terms of a laboratory procedure prescribing harm to a nonhuman animal or a human being. The victim is anesthetized so that her pain during the operation is suppressed. But does the fact that the victim cannot feel the injury the experimenter is inflicting mean that the victim does not suffer the injury? Obviously not, as shown by our primary use of the word "pain" to mean a sensation of hurt, whereas the word "suffering" emphasizes the bearing of it. Thus, while it may be possible to harm an individual in a way that is technically painless—as long as anesthesia is applied during and after the operation—it is not possible to do so in a way that will avoid causing the individual to suffer, that is, to bear the burden of an injury that may include death. This routs the claim made by researchers, for instance, that driving electrodes into the brains of animals, after injecting them with drugs to induce a resemblance to Parkinson's disease prior to killing them, doesn't cause the animals to suffer. If, in discussions of these topics, concepts such as "humane slaughter" were placed in the category of *humane harm*, the impertinence of many seemingly reasonable proposals involving the use of animals would be clear.

The Sickness unto Death and Banality of Evil

But is it possible to suffer without feeling pain in conditions other than physical? The philosopher Kierkegaard argued that despair—the moral condition of hopelessness—is the most profound human suffering there is. He called this painless moral and spiritual suffering "the sickness unto death"

(Bretall). Kierkegaard insisted that, paradoxical as it may seem, an individual and even a whole society can suffer from the sickness of despair without knowing it, that is, without feeling it. This is because, as soon as the painful symptoms, such as guilt, are felt, instead of trying to understand the cause, people turn to palliatives—to pain-masking distractions and soothing illusions that mask their actual condition. To be sick in this way is not only to suffer without pain, but to suffer badly and increasingly because of the lack of pain.

This raises one of the central moral dilemmas of our time. A society such as ours, which demands instant relief for everything from mild depression to minor stomach upset, displays staunch fortitude when it comes to the massive pain and suffering we impose on animals for the sake of food and other products. Here, no pain appears to afflict the majority of people, and, as Judith Barad writes regarding society's priorities in which property is worshipped and animal liberation activities are alien, "the masses may take the sinking of an animal testing laboratory executive's yacht more seriously than they take the fact that the laboratory kills 500 animals on a daily basis" (Barad, 175).

To stand outside the accepted order of things must therefore give pause. Consider Roberta Kalechofsky's claim that "Most suffering today, whether of animals or humans, whether it is physiological or the ripping apart of mother and offspring, is at the hands of other humans" (6–7). The evil of everyday life makes traditional images of wickedness seem tame by comparison. Philosopher Hannah Arendt coined the term "banality of evil" to characterize the particular kind of evil expressed by the Nazi war criminal Adolf Eichmann during his trial in Jerusalem in 1961. Eichmann, whose job had been to collect and deport tens of thousands of Jews and other people to death camps, never seemed to grasp to the day he died the nature of his guilt. Arendt summarized Eichmann's view of his responsibility for the mass murders he willingly facilitated: "he had never been a Jew-hater, and he had never willed the murder of human beings. His guilt came from his obedience, and obedience is praised as a virtue" (Arendt 1964, 247).

In Arendt's view, Eichmann told the truth about himself. There was no evidence that he hated his victims or held any firm ideological convictions. Rather, Eichmann was a commonplace man who functioned as normally in Nazi surroundings as he would have done anywhere in a world governed by rules designed to deceive and camouflage the terrible reality in which he painlessly participated, drew a salary, and lived comfortably ("life in Hitler's Germany—for Germans—was far from unpleasant," as Tony Judt reminds us in *The Nation*, 17). Rather than choosing to be morally attentive, Eichmann epitomized the human tendency to seek protection in cliches, stock phrases, and adherence to conventional codes of conduct (Arendt 2003, 479). His thoughtlessness, multiplied by that of thousands of others like him, was, and is, the basis of a totalitarian state.

Nor is a totalitarian state something that can't happen here. In 1962, Stanley Milgram conducted a series of laboratory experiments in which more than half of his subjects willingly obeyed orders to give what they thought were increasingly painful electric shocks to people who were "screaming in pain or whose silence presumably indicated that they had passed out from the experience" (Schnurer, 107). Writing about the legacy of Holocaust resistance and animal liberation activities, Maxwell Schnurer explains how Milgram's experiments "can be read in the context of the Nazi experience":

When it was exposed that hundreds of thousands of average, everyday people had participated in the slaughter of millions of Jews, Romany, Gays, Lesbians, Anarchists, Communists, and other 'undesirables,' thinkers across the globe wondered what would make a person perpetuate such evil onto the suffering face of another person. Milgram suggested that the human personality could not be trusted to respond to ethical situations with compassion. The Nazi experience and his own experiments led Milgram to conclude that there was widespread possibility for evil to be perpetuated even in the United States (Schnurer, 107).

Schnurer explores Milgram's experiments and the Nazi experience in terms of Ellen Langer's concept of mindlessness. Schnurer says that for Milgram, "our values associated with science and the unwillingness to disobey orders are positions of mindlessness. In the case of Nazis, the mindless categorization of Jews and other unwanted races/classes coupled with a hierarchical industrial order created a context in which concentration camps made sense. Participants in the systems of these orders were willing to engage in evil and become complicit with the evil around them because that *was simply the way that the world was*" (Schnurer, 108).

Now that the Nazi concentration camps and death camps have been revealed, and the carefully coordinated train journeys from the ghettos to the gas chambers have been exposed, the American public is aghast that such a monumental horror could have been mounted and sustained in Germany for more than a decade, almost "invisibly" as it were. At the same time, people have been shocked to learn that the German public knew what was happening, or knew enough, but did little or nothing to stop it. Even worse, in many cases they eagerly assisted. For, as Michael Lerner writes, "There was nothing secret about Hitler's plans," and while there is "little question that the Nazis were the indispensable element in organizing the mass murder of the Jews . . . on an experiential level, Jews were equally shocked at how quickly their non-Jewish neighbors abandoned them, refusing to take risks to stand up on their behalf, or even actively betraying them to the Nazis" (48). Likewise, "the Allies did little to save Jews. There was no concerted effort to destroy the death camps, interdict trains bringing Jews to their deaths, or give support for refugees who had managed to get on ships taking them from Europe" (Lerner, 48). The United States was among the countries that turned back refugees.

III.
Gates of Hell

In his essay "At the Gates of Hell: The ALF and the Legacy of Holocaust Resistance," Maxwell Schnurer explains how his initial discomfort, as a Jew, with placing the animal rights movement "in the shadow of the Holocaust" was revised to the point where he would subsequently write sympathetically about animal liberators and their affinity with Holocaust resistance fighters. What convinced Schnurer of the validity of comparing the atrocities was his trip to Krakow, Poland, in October 2002, where he visited the concentration camps and death camps of Auschwitz and Birkenau. At Birkenau, especially, an awareness emerged of which he writes:

> What I could see at Birkenau were the artifacts of a system of destruction that was massive in scale. I had never realized the size of the infrastructure that was needed to control, enslave, and exterminate that many people. There were hundreds of barracks covering square miles of ground fanning out from my gaze, with nothing but desolate wind between them. Long views of barracks juxtaposed against barbed wire were my only guides as I walked across the concentration camp. At the far end of the camp were the remains of the gas chambers and

incinerators. These gas chambers were far away from the public—with a wide zone of exclusion around these two death camps, citizens would never be exposed to the horrors of the camps unless they worked there or were entering to be killed. At this point I began to think about the geographical position of slaughterhouses in America. Kept far away from the public view, the institutions of slaughter in America are equally massive and hidden from sight (Schnurer, 121–122).

As you drive down Route 13 on the Eastern Shore of Maryland into Virginia, as I frequently do, you pass two gigantic chicken slaughter plant operations on your right: first the Tyson Processing Complex, followed several miles down the road by the Perdue Processing Plant. Each of these plants sits discreetly back from the highway with a corporate-window front facing the road and a neutral corporate sign posted in the lawn leading up to the complex. Each is flanked by other buildings and a big, car-filled parking lot. All day long, trucks carrying thousands of baby chickens, packed visibly in crates and cages stacked high on the flatbeds, lumber up and down Route 13, turn into these complexes, drive back out with rickety empty containers, and return with a fresh heaving load of victims. One morning I stood outside the Perdue plant along the highway, and happening to look down at my feet I saw, beaten into the dirt, hundreds of little chicken faces, small decapitated heads and impressions of previous little faces that must have toppled out of the dump trucks as the driver turned the corner to bear these waste objects off to a landfill or rendering plant somewhere.

One late February afternoon, on impulse, I swerve off Route 13 onto the road leading into the Tyson complex, pass the turnstile, and sit in my car with the windows up, gazing at the scene around back. It is an ugly, dirty, desolate sight, the

Gestapo of the human spirit engraved on the landscape. A truckload of chickens sits alone on the dock next to the building where the people inside will kill them, and it will not be a humane death. Apart from some scuttling rubbish and a few seagulls here and there, nothing from where I sit appears to move. The chickens appear silent and still, and no human beings are visible in this moment of understanding, for the umpteenth time, the presumption of being a witness with something to say about another soul's experience of being in hell.

Chapter Three

THE HENMAID'S TALE
The Life of One Battery Hen

Prologue

Sound of a Battery Hen
You can tell me: if you come by the north door,
I am in the twelfth cage
on the left-hand side of the third row
from the floor; and in that cage
I am usually the middle one of eight or six or three.
But even without directions, you'd
discover me. We have the same pale
comb, clipped yellow beak and white or auburn
feathers, but as the door opens and you
hear above the electric fan a kind of
one-word wail, I am the one
who sounds loudest in my head.
—Anonymous

The Incubator
    Deep inside an industrial incubator filled with thousands of
chick embryos, a baby hen is growing inside an egg. During
the first 24 hours after her egg was laid, the chick's tiny heart
started beating, and blood vessels formed that joined her to

the yolk which feeds her as she floats and grows in the fluid of her encapsulated world. Her nervous system began to develop in her twenty-first hour of life inside the incubator, and since her twenty-fourth hour of being there, she has had eyes. By the fourth day, all of her body organs are developed, and by the sixth day, she has the face of a little bird. Her beak has grown, and with it the egg tooth she will use to break out of her shell—the shell that was formed by her mother hen's body, in a breeding facility somewhere—to protect her from harm.

The baby hen has comforting exchanges with the other embryos in the incubator, but a forlornness is felt inside each bird that passes from shell to shell.

The two-way communication between themselves and a mother hen—the continuous interaction which they are genetically endowed to expect, and which they need—has not occurred. The mother hen's heartbeat is missing, and she does not respond to the embryos' calls of distress or comfort them with her soft clucks. The reverberation of something continuously running outside the eggs does not spark meaningful associations, as, for example, the crow of a rooster or the sensation of the hen shifting her eggs with her breast and her beak would comfortingly do.

Still, by the twentieth day, the baby hen occupies all of her egg, except for the air cell, which she now begins to penetrate with her beak, inhaling air through her lungs for the first time. The air isn't fresh, and the baby hen rests for several hours. Then, with renewed energy, she cuts a circular line counterclockwise around the shell by striking it with her egg tooth near the large end of the egg. With this tooth, which disappears after hatching, she saws her way out of the shell. Twelve hours later, wet and exhausted, she emerges to face the life ahead.

"As each chick emerges from its shell in the dark cave of feathers underneath its mother . . . ." But this is not the baby hen's birth

experience. Start over: *"As the mother hen picks the last pieces of shell gently from her chick's soft down . . . ."* But this is not part of the baby hen's story, either. Try again: *"As soon as all the eggs are hatched, the hungry mother hen and her brood go forth to eat, drink, scratch and explore, the baby hen running eagerly within sight and sound of her mother, surrounded by her brothers and sisters."* In reality, none of this happens, except in memories that arise in the baby hen's dreams as she grows and stares through the bars, in the cages that await her arrival.

The "Servicing" Area

The baby hen and her fluffy yellow companions are being wheeled down the hall in the incubator cart. When it stops, three workers remove each tray of newly hatched chicks. They toss, sort and dump the discarded shells, the half-hatched chicks, the deformed chicks and the male chicks into the trash. They smoke cigarettes between the arrival of each cart, and the tobacco fumes along with other odors and gases produce a sickish, burning sensation in the baby hen's eyes, chest and stomach. One of her companions hops onto the edge of the tray and falls to the floor. High-pitched screeches occur as the carts, which now include hers, wheel into the next room, crushing and half crushing the fallen ones, who lie plastered with blood on the floor.

One by one, each chick in the tray is grabbed by a hand and pushed up against a machine blade. Now it's the baby hen's turn, and as her face is pushed against the blade, an agonizing crunch and pain shoots through her beak and her body causing her to flap her wings, cry out, and lose control of her bowels. Smoke and stench mingle as the traumatized chicks, each with a stumped red hole at the front of her face, are sprayed with something chemical, and the baby hen blacks out. She jerks awake upon feeling herself being grabbed and jammed in a cage in a dark place.

The Pullet House

Throbbing pain in her head and her beak, jostling by the other hens, wires hurting her feet, air that makes her sick—the hen can never get comfortable. She cannot obey her impulse to walk and run. She is in a cage in the "pullet" house, where she and the other young hens, thousands of them, will eat mash from the trough, excrete into the manure piles, and grow until, five months later, they are moved to the layer house and into the smaller egg-laying cages. The hen and rooster who created her in the breeding facility were slaughtered while she was still in the incubator. Her brothers were suffocated at the hatchery, and she has sisters somewhere, perhaps in the same building that she's living in.

She suffers excruciating pain when she accidentally bumps her wounded beak several times against the metal trough when she tries to eat the mash. Her body aches, her heart beats in fear, her face is disfigured, things crawl on her skin. There is no earth to bathe in. Healing, her beak develops small bulbs, called neuromas, and in time the pain almost stops, just a dull ache there, but the young hen can never preen herself properly, or eat right, although she tries, and when she and some other hens appear in a magazine picture, people who never knew her think that she and her sad companions are ugly by nature.

The Layer House

One night a hand flings her out of the pullet cage, into another cage, and wheels her to a third cage. Feelings pass between herself and the other hens pressing against her, as their combs grow white and lumpy and hang over their eyes like dough, but no words exist for these feelings, just as there is nothing in the natural evolution of hens to prepare them for this situation. When a cagemate dies and rots, the hen stands on top of her to get off the wires. Her cage is somewhere among stacks and rows of cages. She is in a universe of cages. Eggs form in her body, are expelled with difficulty, and roll away. Rats whisk through the troughs, leaving pellets in the mash. They whisk in and out of the cage bars, even brush through her feathers, which are mostly broken spines now. Flies suck stray yolks in the aisle in front of her cage, and one day the troughs are empty.

The End

Somehow the hen has managed to get her head and one spiny wing stuck between the bars of her cage, and she can't free herself. Ignorant people say that a chicken doesn't know she is going to die, but the hen knows that she is going to die. When a hand—the most brutal, cruel thing she knows—opens the cage door and pulls her backward from inside, yanking her almost in two, she shrieks as she is dropped into the bucket where other hens, oozing eggs, pieces of shells and blood await her. They absorb her into themselves, as something heavy and soft plops on top of her that moves just a little, or so she feels, in being carried away.

Chapter Four

HOLOCAUST VICTIMIZATION IMAGERY

" . . . the ready-made modern example of hell on earth."
—A. Alvarez

As other experiences functioned as figures for the Holocaust, shaping comprehension and expression of specific events, the Holocaust itself would now function as a guiding figure for other events, especially the realities of inner life that are possibly generated by knowledge of the Holocaust.—**James E. Young**, *Writing and Rewriting the Holocaust*

Two primary negative assumptions arise for consideration in the case for comparing atrocities. One is that no one can truly enter into the pain and suffering of another. To assume otherwise amounts to a kind of arrogance or well-meaning ignorance with respect to the unbridgeable laws of trespass and inviolability of each individual, each collective entity, each episode of pain. The other is that the suffering of a particular individual or group cannot be objectively compared with that of another. Each episode of pain is incommensurable, and, as such, it cannot be extrapolated. Needless to say, if each episode of pain and suffering is unique and unknowable to all but the primary sufferer, the whole idea of comparing atrocities—the very idea of vicarious experience—vanishes.

Clearly these assumptions present difficulties: on the one

hand people want others to understand their suffering. On the other hand the very presumption of understanding may strike the victim as an insult, one more wound added to all the others. But more than understanding is involved, for above all, people want their suffering to have meaning. Victims of atrocity want their experience to have both private and public meaning—meaning inscribed, through sharable public images and discourse, in the mind of an audience composed of those very outsiders "who can never understand." But if understanding is precluded, the question arises as to what meaning or meanings, if any, can possibly be shared. How can meaning be imparted and shared in a context of events that are conceived by their very nature as discrete and dissociated from one another?

Say for instance that a person who is not Jewish and who was not a Holocaust survivor nevertheless sees his or her own suffering figured in the light of the Holocaust. Say that for this person, the Holocaust replicates certain specific internal themes in such a way as to allow those themes to be articulated and linked to the larger community of life rather than suffered in isolation. James E. Young points out that for certain individuals, be they Jewish or non-Jewish, the Holocaust may figure as a reflection of inner realities. It may even be a cause of painful internal suffering (125). Regarding the reciprocity of such outer and inner realities, Young speaks of "the inevitability of knowing each in terms of the other" (124).

Sylvia Plath's "Right" to Holocaust Imagery

Young explores these ideas in his discussion of the controversy surrounding the poet Sylvia Plath's metaphorical use of Holocaust victimization imagery to characterize her own psychology of oppression via her poetry. It has been alleged against Plath, who was not Jewish, that, in the words of Edward Butscher: "There is no way that the poetry of an American girl writing from the remote perspective of the 1950s could ever capture the actual brutal reality of the Holocaust" (Young, 117–118). However, Young says that Plath was not literally trying to capture the Holocaust. The question, he believes, is not Plath's "right" to Holocaust imagery but, rather, "how the Holocaust—once it became its own archetype and entered the public imagination as an independent icon— also became a figure for subsequent pain, suffering, and destruction" (118). Young explains:

> As long as these images of the Holocaust are public, they inevitably enter the private imagination at some level, where they are invariably evoked to order personal experience. To use the camp experience as a "ready-made modern example" (Alvarez's words) of one's personal pain need not be a conscious or deliberate act, but only a way of knowing one's inner life in the language and figures of an outer world (121).

The question may accordingly be asked how the Holocaust could become a figure for the preexisting pain and destruction of other individuals and groups, including other species, through vicarious representation. If realities of the inner life can be generated by knowledge of the Holocaust, so, perhaps, the Holocaust may provide a way not only to characterize the suffering of nonhuman animals, but also to characterize the sorrow of people who suffer empathically with animals imprisoned in laboratories and zoos and on factory farms. For some people, knowing what animals endure at the hands of human beings is itself a kind of "eternal Treblinka." In *Science, Animals, and Evolution*, Catherine Roberts presents the view, for example, that "many more people than is generally supposed suffer at the thought of what goes one in laboratories, and still more would become extremely agitated and uneasy in their minds if they knew of the atrocities of the extreme forms of animal experimentation" (Roberts, 104).

According to Young, criticism of Sylvia Plath's use of Holocaust victimization imagery goes beyond the charge that her figures are exploitative and disproportionate. It has been said that neither she nor anyone else who "wasn't there" has the right to export Holocaust images outside the literal Holocaust milieu. George Steiner asks whether anyone other than an actual survivor has "the right to put on this death-rig?" To which Young replies: "no more so than any of us has the right to compare our lot with that of the Jews escaping Egypt, or the destruction of cities in wartime with that of Jerusalem in 587 BCE. We do not put on these 'death-rigs' because they fit, but because they are remembered archetypes in our language by which we grasp our current lives" (130).

In defending Sylvia Plath's use of Holocaust victimization imagery to characterize her own inner suffering, which she linked to recent and current public events including Dachau, Hiroshima, and the horrific execution by electrocution of Julius and Ethel Rosenberg, "burned alive all along [their] nerves" (Plath, 1), Young shows how Holocaust Jews them-selves drew upon their own repository of language and biblical narrative to characterize, organize, and give meaning to the otherwise colossal chaos of horror they endured, including the sense of being not just stateless, but cut off from human con-cern altogether (Young, 120, 124). In the words of Bruno Bettelheim: "What happened to them impressed on them that nobody cared whether they lived or died, and that the rest of the world, including foreign countries, had no concern for their fate" (Bettelheim, 102).

Lesser Evils

By dint of an indefatigable effort on the part of the Jewish community, the victims of the Holocaust are no longer forgotten. Jewish writers have impressed the Holocaust on the mind of Western culture to such an extent that all other atrocities now fall under the shadow of the Holocaust as "lesser evils." In "The Perils of Indifference," Elie Wiesel offers the perspective that he helped to create on the "failures" of the twentieth century. "These failures," he says, "have cast a dark shadow over humanity: two World Wars, countless civil wars, the senseless chain of assassinations (Gandhi, the Kennedys, Martin Luther King, Sadat, Rabin), bloodbaths in Cambodia and Nigeria, India and Pakistan, Ireland and Rwanda, Eritrea and Ethiopia, Sarajevo and Kosovo; the inhumanity in the gulag and the tragedy of Hiroshima. And, on a different level, of course, Auschwitz and Treblinka" (Wiesel).

But how, exactly, are Auschwitz and Treblinka "on a different level"—inherently as opposed to the place they occupy in Western social consciousness—from all those other horrors? This is not to say that they should be lumped together, but to inquire whether the Holocaust should assume the aspect of Mt. Everest with respect to every other atrocity, past, present, and future. This is a difficult question, in part because among those who challenge the privileging of the Holocaust to the point of unavailability for further application are people who invoke the Holocaust to illuminate other overwhelming atrocities. But the reason is clear. In our cultural era, the Holocaust has become the paradigmatic symbol for mass, anonymous, innocent suffering imposed by stupendous inhumanity—"the ready-made modern example of hell on earth." The Holocaust's only rival, judging from the figure most commonly invoked to capture the Holocaust experience, is the suffering of nonhuman animals. Time and again, the suffering of animals is pulled from oblivion to evoke ineffable human horror as the ready-made example of hell on earth.

However, the appropriation of animal suffering to express human suffering is seldom accorded the justice of reciprocity.

On the contrary, at the time of this writing, many Jewish people have expressed indignation over comparisons that are being made by animal advocates between the human-imposed suffering endured by billions of nonhuman animals each year and the suffering endured by millions of Jews under the Nazis. My own stance on the issue appeared in a 1999 profile of my work in *The Washington Post*. In "For the Birds," *Washington Post* writer Tamara Jones declared at the outset: "Yes, Karen Davis is serious when she says the extermination of 7 billion broiler chickens is the moral equivalent of the Holocaust" (F1). After publication of the article, I received a voice-mail message denouncing my stance as anti-Semitic, even though the article stressed how my preoccupation with the evils perpetrated on innocent victims under Hitler had evolved to illuminate my awareness of humanity's relentless institutionalized assault upon nonhuman animals (Jones 1999, F5).

Invoking the Pain of Others

Resentment of comparisons between the suffering of the Jews and the suffering of nonhuman animals in conditions of atrocity is not an isolated attitude. It is part of a broader human psychology of resentment at having one's suffering compared with that of anyone else, for, as Susan Sontag says in her book, *Regarding the Pain of Others*, "It is intolerable to have one's own sufferings twinned with anybody else's" (113). Sontag does not include animals in her book on the iconography of suffering or submit her particular claim about the intolerability of "twinned" suffering to analysis. She does, however, cite the reaction of the Sarajevans to a photo gallery of their plight that included images of the plight of the Somalians. "For the Sarajevans, it was . . . simple. To set their sufferings alongside the sufferings of another people was to compare them (which hell was worse?), demoting Sarajevo's martyrdom to a mere instance. The atrocities taking place in Sarajevo have nothing to do with what happens in Africa, they exclaimed" (Sontag, 113).

Two important issues emerge from Sontag's analysis. First, members of an oppressed group often resent comparisons of their suffering with members of another oppressed group because they believe that the analogy demotes their suffering from something unique to "a mere instance" of generic suffering. Second, a group may feel that their suffering is actually more important than that of any other group. The question of just comparisons between or among different groups is important, since it is not just any suffering, but the unjust, deliberately imposed suffering one's group has already endured (suffering intentionally imposed by humans as opposed to suffering incurred in the wake of a natural disaster such as an earthquake) which adds to the resentment one feels in having to protect one's own group experience from appropriation by another group. The original injustice should not be compounded by the further injustice of being used, in Richard Kahn's words, merely as "an emblem for more pressing matters" (Kahn).

Treatment versus Experience

In a letter to the editor, an indignant writer justifies using animals to express human Holocaust suffering, but not the reverse: "Yes, the Nazis treated us like animals, maybe worse than animals," she writes. "But it's just an expression we use" (Jacobs). It is acceptable, in other words, to appropriate the treatment of nonhuman animals to characterize one's own mistreatment, but not the other way around. Advocates of this position believe that they can legitimately use the experience of nonhuman animals to characterize their own experience, even when the animals' experience has not been duly acknowledged or imaginatively conceived of to any degree, and perhaps has been dismissed without further inquiry. If so, it may be asked why anyone would compromise the case for the incomparability of one's own suffering by comparing it to the suffering of animals, given that nonhuman animals and their suffering are regarded as vastly inferior.

But it is precisely the distinction between "treatment" and "experience" that fuels the resentment. To be "treated like animals" is an insult because the experience of animals is assumed to be vastly inferior to that of any human being, most of all one's particular group. The worth of animals has traditionally been regarded as instrumental worth only. "Animals were put on earth for humans to use" is the standard formula, with "responsibly" or "humanely" tacked on as an afterthought. Presuming an immeasurable gulf between humans and animals allows one to appropriate animal abuse as a metaphor for one's own mistreatment while simultaneously dismissing the metaphor, and hence the "animals," as "just an expression." In this figure of speech, the term "animal" has no concrete or independent meaning even as "animal." It is simply a code word for "humans badly treated by other humans," though not necessarily in a sense that is troubling to the speaker, who may be as likely to dismiss the suffering of nonhuman animals with another formula, "They're only animals."

Animal Genocide

The concept of genocide has been used to discredit the idea of an animal holocaust. Objecting to the title of Charles Patterson's book, *Eternal Treblinka*, a writer argues that a factory farm "can be cruel and brutal, but it is not a 'Treblinka'" (Oboler). The concentration camps, he writes, "were designed to exterminate all Jewish men, women, and children wherever they may be," whereas a factory farm "is not designed to exterminate all animals wherever they may be. It is designed to cruelly and brutally exploit animals for profit. In fact, killing all animals would defeat their purpose. It is therefore wrong and offensive to compare a concentration camp designed for the genocide of an entire people with a factory farm" (Oboler).

Not until I began writing this book did I have a different idea of genocide from the one given above. That is, I understood genocide to refer exclusively to the direct killing or attempted direct killing of every member of a human group with the goal of physically destroying that group and its presence on earth. Ward Churchill's book *A Little Matter of Genocide: Holocaust and Denial in the Americas 1492 to the Present*, broadened my understanding. The term genocide was originally formulated by the Polish jurist Raphael Lemkin in his 1944 book, *Axis Rule in Occupied Europe*. According to Churchill, "Lemkin makes it absolutely clear from the outset that his concept of genocide was never meant to pertain exclusively to direct killing, this being but one means to the end of destroying the *identity* of targeted groups" (Churchill 1997, 70).

In an effort to characterize what was happening to the Jews, Gypsies, Slavs and other victim groups under the Nazis, Lemkin wrote that genocide has two phases: "one, destruction of the national pattern of the oppressed group; the other, the imposition of the national pattern of the oppressor. The imposition, in turn, may be made upon the oppressed population which is allowed to remain, or upon the territory alone, after removal of the population and colonization of the area by the oppressor's own nationals" (Lemkin quoted in Churchill 1997, 68).

This concept of genocide allows us to consider humanity's relentless, wholesale assault on the individuals, families, and communities of other animal species as a "genocidal" project both in its own right and in the context of organized genocidal assaults by human populations on one another. Just as it makes sense to speak of a "genocidal relationship implemented through racism" in the case of America's aggression in Southeast Asia, for example (Sartre quoted in Churchill 1997, 416), so it makes sense to speak of genocidal relationships implemented through speciesism in the myriad examples of humankind's conquest of nonhuman animals and their living space.

The destruction and/or relocation and exile of countless animal species and remnant populations of animals, under the assertion of the human "right" to possess and impose its pattern on them and the land they inhabit (or inhabited), corresponds to the European colonial assault on the native human inhabitants of the African and American continents. It parallels the Nazi territorial expansionism known as *Lebensraumpolitik* (Churchill 1997, 421). The Nazi politics of "must have" living space was an extension of the territorial expansionism boasted by the United States in the nineteenth century as its "manifest destiny" of conquering the Southwest and the Northwest, and islands in the Pacific and Caribbean, following its previous and continuing depredations and exterminations in South and Central America.

The Nazi concept of "living space," as Enzo Traverso writes in *The Origins of Nazi Violence*, "was simply the German version of a commonplace of European culture at the time of imperialism" (51). This commonplace, which "postulated a hierarchy in the right to existence," consisted in "the principle of the West's right to dominate the world, to colonize the planet, and to subjugate or even eliminate 'savage peoples.' Where colonization involved the total eradication of native populations, as in the United States," Traverso writes, "that principle was affirmed most explicitly: in 1850, at the height of the stampede to grab lands in the West, the American anthropologist Robert Knox declared in *The Race of Man* that 'extermination' was, quite simply, 'a law of Anglo-Saxon America'" (Traverso, 54).

Expanding this theme, French anthropologist Edmond Perrier wrote in 1888: "Human races owe their spread on earth to their superiority. Just as animals disappear before the advance of man, this privileged being, so too the savage is wiped out before the European, before civilization ever takes hold of him. However regrettable this may be from a moral point of view, civilization seems to have spread throughout the world far more by dint of destroying the barbarians than by subjecting them to its laws" (Perrier quoted in Traverso, 57–58).

Clearly, civilization (so-called) has spread by both of these means. As Lemkin indicated, genocide represents the imposition of the oppressor's pattern of life on the life pattern of an oppressed group ("subjecting the group to its laws"), a process that may, but does not invariably, entail the complete and direct annihilation of the subjugated group, vestiges and deformations of which may remain for shorter or longer periods, despite, or at the behest of, the oppressing agency. Philosopher Jean-Paul Sartre noted, for example, that dependence on the labor of the subject people and the preservation of the colonial economy places restraints on the physical genocide that otherwise tends to proceed where no material advantage is to be gained from restraint. The dependence of the colonizers on the subject people protects them, to a certain extent, from physical genocide, even as "cultural genocide, made necessary by colonialism as an economic system of unequal exchange," continues (Sartre quoted in Churchill, 416). This model of genocide has parallels to the humans-over-nonhuman-animals model of conquest. An example is the maintenance of "theme parks" and zoo populations of animals otherwise targeted for extinction.

Anthropomorphism

Ever since Darwin's theory of evolution erupted in the nineteenth century (*The Origin of Species* appeared in 1859), animal exploiters have invoked the word "anthropomorphism," a term "previously reserved to describe the attribution of human characteristics to the deity" (Ryder, 163), to suppress objections to the cruel and inhumane treatment of animals and to enforce the doctrine of an unbridgeable gap between humans and other animals. The term "anthropomorphism," as it is now used, refers almost entirely to the attribution of consciousness, emotions, and other mental states, commonly regarded as exclusively or predominantly human, to nonhuman animals. The irony of experimenting on animals to learn more about humans while (and by) defending this gap has frequently been noted, as in this 1885 comment by A. Armitt, cited by Richard Ryder: "It is, indeed, the scientists themselves who have proved to us the close relationship existing between man and animals, and their probable development from the same origin. It is they who instruct us to cast aside the old theology which makes men differ from the beasts of the field, inasmuch as he was created in 'the image of God,' and yet would arbitrarily keep, for their own convenience, the line of division which such a belief marked out between man and animals" (Ryder, 163).

In fact, anthropomorphism based on empathy and careful observation is a valid approach to understanding other species, and in any case, we can only see the world "through their eyes" by looking through our own. That said, humans are linked to other animals through evolution, and communication between many species is commonplace. Reasonable inferences can be drawn regarding such things as an animal's body language and vocal inflections in situations that produce comparable responses in humans. Chickens, for example, have a voice of unmistakable woe or enthusiasm in situations where these responses make sense. Their body language of "curved toward the earth" (drooping) versus "head up, tail up" is similarly interpretable. As in comparing atrocities, behavioral resemblances don't require an exact match. One may consider these resemblances in terms of the common wellspring from which all experience flows, or in the form of a musical analogy, as in the theme of sentience and its innumerable manifestations harking back to the matrix of all sentient forms.

Anthropomorphism conceived in these terms makes sense. One may legitimately formulate ideas about animals and their needs that the rhetoric of exploitation seeks to discredit. One may proffer a counter rhetoric of animal liberation, as when Pattrice Jones warns animal advocates of the danger that in seeing ourselves as the voice for animals, "we can forget to listen to them" (Jones 2004, 151). Jones writes:

> If you have no idea how you might go about taking the opinions of animals into account, that's a sign that you have not paid attention to the problem of how to listen to the animals before attempting to be their voice. Given the limitations of cross-species communication, one must take particular care to learn whatever it is possible to learn about the hopes and fears of the nonhuman animals one hopes to help. There are two intersecting avenues of approach: empathy and observation. Getting to know animals—either by spending time with them or by learning from trustworthy people who have spent time with them—allows one to use empathy accurately. That means asking not "What would I want if I were in a battery cage?" but "What would I want *if I were a chicken* in a battery cage?" Careful observation—either directly or via the factual reports of trustworthy people—allows one to make inferences about animal preferences based on the actions they have taken on their own behalf. That means asking not "What do the experts believe that these animals want?" but "What do the actions of these animals tell anybody willing to listen to what they want?" (Jones 2004, 156)

Even those of us who are working to advance society's view

of animals from beings who merely live to beings who share with us a unique individual and group experience (Guillermo) must beware of our tendency to impose our personal pattern on those we seek to liberate from others' oppression. In the case of the "often unconscious dynamics" of oppression, Jones explains how a pattern of sexist socialization can translate unawares into one of speciesist socialization in which stereotypes of women and animals merge and have superimposed upon them the identities of the dominant group. Jones calls upon animal liberationists to challenge sexism by questioning an ethic in which the natural world and nonhuman animals are reduced to "'damsels in distress' awaiting rescue by the muscular hero." Of course, Jones says, "many captive animals are, indeed, powerless to effect their own escape and thus in need of rescue. Our cultural conditioning makes it very easy for us to slide from that fact into the fantasy of the helpless feminine victim who is entirely dependent on the powerful masculine hero. This, in turn, can lead us to fail to take the animals' own agency and opinions into account when planning our actions on their behalf. Seeing ourselves as their voice, we can forget to listen to them" (Jones 2004, 150–151).

If the tendency to impose one's own identify on others figures even in those who seek to liberate others from oppression, it can come as no surprise that this tendency appears as the speciesist equivalent of genocide under conditions of conquest upheld by the belief that one's own group is superior and has the right to possess and alter whatever can be appropriated and manipulated. With these thoughts, then, let us consider the charge that, in comparing a concentration camp to a factory farm, we err.

Chapter Five

PROCRUSTEAN SOLUTIONS

We cannot presume that animals react to stress and fear in exactly the same manner as humans. Yet if the treatment meted out to factory animals were inflicted on human beings, we could only conceive it to be possible under the most cruel, cynical, and immoral of totalitarian regimes—a thought that brings to mind similarities in the treatment of humans in concentration camps and of animals in confinement. The analogy is plain and undeniable; for both groups are held at the mercy of unfeeling keepers, deprived of freedom, crowded into small spaces, mutilated, tattooed, branded, and permanently marked, subjected to genetic experimentation—and ultimately murdered.—**C. David Coats**, *Old MacDonald's Factory Farm*

. . . animals, so emblematic of delicate, complex organic tissue, surrounded by machines, connected to machines, penetrated by machines in research laboratories or crowded together in space-age facilities . . .—**J. Baird Callicott**, "Animal Liberation: A Triangular Affair"

A state-of-the-art hen house holds 100,000 birds in minuscule cages stretching the length of two football fields; it resembles a late-twentieth-century torture chamber.—**Michael Watts**, "The Age of the Chicken"

"Please, never, ever, call me a battery hen. . . . I am in a battery cage, and I do live on a battery farm. But I am not, repeat not a battery hen. A hen in a battery cage is not a battery hen. Which is to say, she is not some kind of newly-invented species. . . . I, Minny, am a proud descendant of the Red Jungle Fowl."—**Clare Druce**, *Minny's Dream*

In 2004, a professor of agriculture at Dordt College in Sioux Center, Iowa, gave a talk in which he argued that the animal rights movement consists mainly of urbanites with "anthropomorphized visions of animals." Animal rights people, he said, know animals mainly as pets, and having been taught that humans "really are like animals" (O'Rourke, 1567), these people have a sentimentalized view of animals.

In reality, animal users may be more justly accused of anthropomorphism, if by this word is meant the imposition of human traits and impulses on other species in order to justify mistreating them. In cockfighting, for instance, as Pattrice Jones has stressed, roosters are forced to die "in stylized spectacles of masculinity that have nothing to do with natural bird behavior and everything to do with human ideas about gender" (Jones 2004, 141). And what is taking elephants from their natural habitat and sticking them in circuses if not anthropomorphism?

In fairness, philosopher Barbara Noske points out that animal rights people, as well, are liable to try to turn nonhuman animals into "duplicates of themselves," surrounded as so many of us are "by machines in an entirely humanized, electronic techno-world" (Noske 2004, 3). As urban dwellers encountering animals who are "made to live (and die) in human-manufactured habitats" (1), animal advocates may be tempted to portray animals as if they were "isolated, city-dwelling consumer-citizens, living entirely outside of any ecological context" (3). An example is the attempt by some advocates to turn their carnivorous companion animals into vegans. Noske questions whether this is about "protecting companion animals from non-ethical food or about imposing human ethics on the animal other?" In addition, she cites the ethical dilemma that even "much plant-based and processed food happens to be the end-product of unsustainable monocultures—to which many animal habitats have had to give way—and has been put on the market by the same globalized and diversified agro-industrial complex which also produces standard pet foods" (Noske 2004, 2).

In contrast to the animal advocate's potentially overzealous "humanization" of companion animals, the so-called circus elephant and fighting cock exemplify the kind of anthropomorphism on which animal exploiters depend. It consists of insisting that animals they want to use are happy or not suffering in being exploited, despite a congeries of evidence to the contrary. Nor is this conclusion a mere animal rights fantasy, as there is plenty of scientific evidence to support the claims and concerns of animal advocates. Poultry welfare specialist Ian Duncan, of the University of Guelph in Ontario, states, for example, that chickens and turkeys bred for meat "represent welfare problems on a huge scale." By welfare, Duncan explains, "I mean 'what animals feel,' including pain, frustration, and fear and how these feelings relate to genetic fitness and the environment" (Duncan, 2). He cites, for example, the condition known as "ascites syndrome," a cardiovascular-oxygen deficiency disease in "broiler" chickens in which fluid accumulates in the body, causing the bird to suffocate.

In addition, Duncan notes that "skeletal problems are increasing in meat-type chickens and turkeys, which isn't surprising."

While in the 1950s it took 12 weeks to raise a five-pound chicken, the time has been reduced to 6 weeks, at enormous cost to the birds. These birds are all extremely unfit. In treadmill experiments, for example, their core body temperature goes up abnormally high. There is also the interaction between their unfitness and their poor environment. The poultry environment is full of dust and ammonia which get into the birds' lungs. Ammonia destroys the cilia that would otherwise prevent harmful bacteria from being inhaled. As a result, the birds develop respiratory infections such as airsacculitis. They are inhaling harmful bacteria constantly (Duncan, 2).

Likewise, poultry welfare specialist Joy Mench, of the University of California-Davis, describes the suffering of chickens raised for meat and eggs in these terms:

Eight billion broiler chickens and 300 million laying hens are in US agribusiness production each year, with hundreds of thousands, even millions, of birds on a single farm. In this gigantic system individual birds have little value: a whole broiler chicken is worth $4 and the yearly output of 250 eggs per hen amounts to $30. More than 99 percent of US laying hens are in cages, averaging eight hens per cage. Hens in cages develop osteoporosis because they get no exercise and because their limited calcium is mobilized for constant eggshell formation instead of bones (Mench, 1).

The fact is that the needs and desires of animals and the wishes and desires of animal users seldom coincide, so a procrustean solution is sought whereby the animal, and the argument, is, so to speak, either cut down to size or stretched to fit the agenda. In literature, Procrustes, who mutilated his victims so they would fit in his bed, is a symbol of tyranny and cruelly enforced order (Davis 2004, 30). He is thus a fit symbol of the false anthropomorphism in which animals are forced to conform to human constructions that are alien and inimical to animals, whereby they sustain a genocidal assault on their identity.

II.
Extinction through Incarceration

At the heart of the zoo's paradoxical status is a sort of double alienation. On the one hand the zoo is a sort of prison—a space of confinement and a site of enforced marginalization like the penitentiary or the concentration camp. And on the other it cannot subvert the awful reality that the animals, from whatever vantage point they are viewed, are "rendered absolutely marginal." It demonstrates, as Berger is at pains to point out, a basic ecological fact of loss and exclusion—the disappearance and extinction of animals—through an act of incarceration.—**Michael Watts**, "The Age of the Chicken"

In "Why Look at Animals," John Berger presents the environment of the zoo as a paradigm of false anthropomorphism at its worst. The space that modern, institutionalized animals inhabit, Berger writes, "is artificial."

In some cages the light is equally artificial. In all cases the environment is illusory. Nothing surrounds [the animals] except their own lethargy or hyperactivity. They have nothing to act upon—except, briefly, supplied food and—very occasionally—a supplied mate. (Hence their perennial actions become marginal actions without an object.) Lastly, their dependence and isolation have so conditioned their responses that they treat

> any event which takes place around them ---usually it is
> in front of them, where the public is—as marginal.
> (Hence their assumption of an otherwise exclusively
> human attitude—indifference.) . . . At the most, the ani-
> mal's gaze flickers and passes on. They look sideways.
> They look blindly beyond. They scan mechanically.
> They have been immunized to encounter, because noth-
> ing can any more occupy a *central* place in their atten-
> tion (Berger, 286–287).

Berger says that animals in the zoo "disappoint" the public,
especially the children, who want to know, "Where is he? Why
doesn't he move? Is he dead?" Animals on factory farms and
in laboratories differ from animals in the zoo in that they are
not intended to be viewed, yet all of these animals share the
fate of being prevented from being seen in their own right.
Animals on display are the objects of blind, and blinding,
encounters between a human audience and the animals'
human-imposed personas. Animals who break out of their
phony images are punished (further punished, that is, since
the condition of spectacular captivity—captivity for the sake
of spectacle—is, of itself, the fundamental punishment) by
being beaten, starved, isolated, sold, killed, or all of the above.
Zoo animals, so-called, are imprisoned in a world that express-
es elements in human nature that no normal nonhuman animal would voluntarily consent to enter and live in.

Likewise, animals on factory farms are imprisoned in a
world which their psyches did not emanate and which they
accordingly do not understand. Forcing our psychic pattern on
animals who fit the pattern only by being "stretched" or
"amputated" to conform is the very essence of the genocidal
assault on nonhuman animal identity that, in addition to the
direct extermination of millions of animals every day by
humans, forms one of the strongest links to the experience of

the Jews under the Nazis. As Roberta Kalechofsky writes concerning the victimization of both Jews and animals: "Like the Jew," the animal is trapped in the "symbolism of another group. The animal's life and destiny are under the control of the symbolic signs of others" (Kalechofsky, 55).

Factory-farmed animals are imprisoned in total confinement buildings within global systems of confinement, and are thus separated from the natural world in which they evolved. They are imprisoned in alien bodies genetically manipulated for food traits alone, bodies that in many cases have been surgically altered as well, creating a disfigured appearance—they are debeaked, de-toed, dehorned, ear-cropped, tail-docked, castrated, and (in the case of piglets) dentally mutilated—and always without painkillers.

Factory-farmed animals are imprisoned in a belittling concept of who they are. Nor is their predicament new so much as a further turn of the screw that, with genetic engineering and other refinements of unrestrained scientific violence to animals firmly in place, continues to turn. In *The Animal Estate: The English and Other Creatures in the Victorian Age*, Harriet Ritvo shows how animals became surrogates for nineteenth-century agendas, in particular Britain's imperial enterprise in which "material animals" and "rhetorical animals" embodied the most powerful possible symbol of human possession and control:

> As material animals were at the complete disposal of human beings, so rhetorical animals offered unusual opportunities for manipulation; their positions in the physical world and in the universe of discourse were mutually reinforcing. Their ubiquity made animals particularly available to the Victorians, either in the flesh or as something to talk about. They figured prominently in the experience even of city dwellers. The streets were full of cabhorses and carthorses; flocks of sheep

and herds of cattle were driven to market once or twice a week; many urbanites raised pigs and chickens in crowded tenements, or bred a variety of pets, from pigeons to rabbits to fighting dogs. Although these creatures might be strong in the muscular sense, they were also manifestly powerless, as were bulls in rural fields, lions in menageries, and even the dangerous game stalked by hunters on the African plains or in the Indian hills. And in the rhetorical sphere they were less potent still. If the power of discourse lies in its inevitable restructuring and re-creation of reality, the ability of human beings to offer counterinterpretations places inevitable limits on the exercise of that power. Animals, however, never talk back.

The many separate animal-related discourses of nineteenth-century England constituted a single larger unit, which both discussed and exemplified a central theme of domination and exploitation (Ritvo, 5–6).

Marxist Analysis of Factory-Farmed Chickens

In *Humans and Other Animals: Beyond the Boundaries of Anthropology*, Barbara Noske presents a Marxist perspective on humankind's relentless genocidal assault on the identity of nonhuman animals and the false anthropomorphism of factory farming. She argues that nonhuman animals should be regarded with humans as "total beings whose relations with their physical and social environment are of vital importance" (Noske 1989, 18). The morality of forcing human beings to subsist in alien environments to serve economic objectives was analyzed by Karl Marx in terms that provide insight into the experience of chickens, for example, who are shunted into human-created environments that are alien to their nature, a nature that is rooted in the wild jungle fowl of southeast Asia. Marx described four interrelated aspects of alienation: from the product, from the productive activity, from the species life, and from fellow humans. We can look at chickens and other captive animals from a similar viewpoint (Davis 1996, 21–22).

Factory-farmed chickens are alienated from their own products, which consist of their eggs, their chicks, and parts of their own bodies. The eggs of chickens used for breeding are taken away to be artificially incubated and hatched in mechanized hatcheries, and those of caged laying hens roll onto a conveyer belt out of sight. Parents and progeny are dismembered from one another. Factory-farmed chickens live and die without ever knowing a mother hen or the attentive parenting of a rooster. The relationship between the chicken and his or her own body is perverted and degraded by factory farming. An example is the cruel conflict in young broiler chickens between their abnormally rapid accumulation of breast muscle tissue and a developing young skeleton that cannot cope with the growth rate and overweight, resulting in crippling, painful hip joint degeneration and other afflictions that prevent the bird from walking normally, and often, or finally, from walking at all. Just as Nazi concentration camp victims were physically brutalized and denied pain relief medication by their captors, so every day, by the millions, are these chickens.

Factory-farmed chickens are alienated from their own productive activity, which is reduced to the single biological function of laying eggs, producing semen, or gaining weight at the expense of the whole bird. Normal species activity is prevented so that food (energy) will be converted into this particular function only and not be "wasted." Exercise of the chicken's natural repertoire of interests and behaviors conflicts fundamentally with the goals of factory farming.

Factory-farmed chickens are alienated from their own societies. Their species life is distorted by crowding and caging, by separation of parents and offspring, by the huge numbers of birds crowded into vast confinement buildings, and by the lack of natural contact with other age groups and sexes within the species. By nature, chickens should be living in small groups within larger flocks that spend their day actively foraging, dustbathing, sunbathing, socializing and raising their young in a sunlit, forested habitat.

In the most encompassing sense, factory-farmed chickens are alienated from surrounding nature, from an external world that answers intelligibly to their inner world. There is nothing for them to do or see or look forward to, no voluntary actions are permitted, no joy or zest of living. They just have to *be*, in an excremental void, until we kill them. The deterioration of mental and physical alertness that occurs under these circumstances has been rationalized by some animal scientists as an adaptive mechanism preventing further suffering. In *Animals in the Third Reich*, Boria Sax "hopefully" opines that "many animals in industrial farms may be so brutalized by the combination of genetic manipulation and lack of stimulation that they lose the capacity to suffer very much" (167). But as F. Wemelsfelder explains, "It would be conceptually meaningless to assume that such states could in any way come to be experienced by an animal as 'normal' or 'adapted.' Behavioural flexibility represents the very capacity to achieve well-being or adaptation; impairment of such capacity presumably leaves an animal in a helpless state of continuous suffering" (Wemelsfelder, 122).

III.
Forced Labor and Factory Farming

Animal suffering and hatred for the Jew come closest in the industrial complex where animals are reduced to machines. Contempt and abuse are the inevitable consequences of those in power over the powerless in this setting. "Life unworthy of life" and life deemed useful for life elicit similar responses in the bleak utilitarianism of the industrial world.—**Roberta Kalechofsky**, *Animal Suffering and the Holocaust: The Problem with Comparisons*

Unless they were productive, their lives were worthless to their masters.—**Anne Applebaum**, *Gulag: A History*

A primary difference between a factory farm and a concentration camp would seem, at first glance, to be the role played by forced labor. "Work was the central function of most Soviet camps," Anne Applebaum writes in *Gulag: A History*. "It was the main occupation of prisoners, and the main preoccupation of the administration. Daily life was organized around work, and the prisoners' well-being depended upon how successfully they worked" (Applebaum, 217). Hitler built camps to terrorize the German population into compliance with Nazi plans and, after the war broke out, to provide German industry with cheap, expendable labor. Others—the death camps—replaced the mass production of merchandise and armaments with the industrial production and elimination of corpses. But regardless of what they were designed for, as historian Enzo Traverso writes, "The entire existence of Nazi concentration camps was marked by a constant tension between work and extermination. Initially designed as punitive centers, then, during the war, transformed into centers of production, they became de facto centers of extermination through work" (34).

Extermination through Work

Contrary to what we usually think of as "work"—physical and/or mental effort exerted to do or make something—the notion of the "work" of chickens on a factory farm may seem strange. Granted, "egg-laying" hens are caged in horrible conditions, but while they are there, aren't they just laying eggs the way apples fall from a tree? And while chickens raised for meat have been forced to become, in Michael Watts' words, wretched "sites of accumulation" (13), how does becoming buried in one's own flesh constitute work or anything that could reasonably be regarded as forced labor?

If this seems a stretch, consider Watts's imagery in his essay "The Age of the Chicken," where he writes that "the 'designer chicken' establishes the extent to which nutritional and genetic sciences have produced a 'man made' broiler, a cyborg, to fit the needs of industry." There is "something grotesque," Watts argues, "about the creation of a creature which is a sort of steroidally enhanced growth machine, producing in unprecedentedly short periods of time enormous quantities of flesh around a distorted skeleton. . . . What is striking about the chicken is the extent to which the 'biological body' has been actually *constructed* physically to meet the needs of the industrial labor process" (15–16).

Watts does not exaggerate. In the twentieth century the domesticated chicken was divided through genetic research into two separate utility strains, two separate "divisions of labor," if you will, one designed for egg production, the other for meat production. The model of the chicken, in both cases, is based on machine metaphors derived from industrial technology. Factory-farmed chickens are not only *in* factories; they are regarded by the chicken industry *as* factories. The hen, originally a wild jungle fowl, and once an archetype of motherhood, has been converted, economically and rhetorically, to an "egg-laying machine." If hens spoke human language, they would say with the women whose value in Margaret Atwood's book *The Handmaid's Tale* resides solely in their reproductive organs, "We are containers, it's only the insides of our bodies that are important"; and of their captors, they would agree: "They didn't care what they did to your feet or your hands. . . . For [their] purposes your feet and your hands are not essential" (Atwood, 91, 96).

The forced labor of chickens on factory farms is internalized forced labor. Like everything else in their lives, including their lives, the work imposed on these birds is invisible. This is because, in addition to its being conducted inside total confinement buildings, the work has been built into the chicken's genome with the result that the bird's body is locked in a state of perpetual warfare with itself and with the essential nature of the chicken as such. A former chicken farmer captures something of the cruel and unnatural burden embedded within these birds when she writes that "the sign of a good meat flock is the number of birds dying from heart attacks" (Baskin, 38).

Factory-farmed chickens are designed not only to be slaughtered at extremely young ages, but to die prematurely regardless. They are forced to produce too many eggs if they are "laying" hens and to generate, from the overstrained pumping of their hearts, too much muscle tissue if they are "broiler" chickens. Industry sources say that hens used for egg production are so overwrought that they exhibit the "emotionality" of "hysteria," and that something as simple as an electrical storm can produce "an outbreak of hysteria" in four-to-eight-week-old "broiler" chickens (Bell and Weaver, 89; Clark, et al., 2). The nihilism of the human psyche has thus been pathologically projected into the body of the chicken. The enemy—Man—is incorporated in the chicken as an alien being representing the negation of the chicken's own form of existence.

The impregnation of the chicken with human traits and desires starts in the genetics laboratory, but it doesn't stop there. Experimental "research" on chickens is conducted in privately owned and publicly funded laboratories throughout the world. Chickens are used in basic research, biomedical research, toxicity research, and agricultural research. There are no restraints on what may be done to chickens in this universe of assault, just as there "were no restraints in what the SS felt they could do in the concentration camps" to human prisoners (Kalechofsky, 29). Following are some examples gleaned from thousands of experiments (Davis 2003):

- In a research project funded by H. Ross Perot, Dr. Mohamed Abou-Donia, a professor of pharmacology and neurobiology and deputy director of Duke University Medical Center's Toxicity Program, did a study in 1994–1995, designed to "mimic doses" of anti-nerve-gas pills and insecticides such as DEET (Diethyltoluamide Metadelphene) used by soldiers during the Gulf War. Over 100 chickens were exposed to either the anti-nerve-gas pill or to commonly used insecticides, such as DEET, or to combinations of the two. Chickens exposed to combinations of the chemicals "died or displayed nervous system effects such as weakness, difficulty walking, ataxia and paralysis." Perot said "several government agencies and the Pentagon had been in contact with him about the test results." ("Death, Nerve Damage")
- A researcher whose experiment consisted of shaving hens naked with sheep shears in heat-stress experiments for the egg industry said that shaving the hens naked was "very humane, just like a haircut" (Coon; Peguri and Coon).
- Q. "Can you give an example of the kind of research you did?" A. "Yes. I knew that wings and tails of birds were unnecessary to commercial production of poultry meat, so I did research to show that a grower could save about 15 percent of feed costs by cutting off the tails and wings of broiler chickens and turkey poults soon after hatching. I gave papers on that at national meetings, and attracted a great deal of interest" (Davis 1996, 88–89).
- In a study published in *Poultry Science* in 1984, researchers in the Poultry Science Department, Alabama Agricultural Experiment Station, and Veterinary Diagnostic Laboratory at the University of Auburn manually inserted inflated balloons, shell membranes, and tampons into the uteri of hens

and gave them inflammatory and immunosuppressive drugs to determine "possible causes of shell-less eggs, a multimillion dollar loss to US egg producers." The presence of these objects in the hens' uteri caused high fever, vomiting, diarrhea, and death (Roland).

- In 2002, Avigdor Cahaner, a professor of quantitative genetics at Hebrew University's Faculty of Agricultural, Food and Environmental Quality Sciences, announced his creation of a featherless chicken. He said the bird is designed to withstand mass production temperatures in the hot climates in the Middle East and thus eliminate the need for expensive cooling systems for raising poultry in such places. Cahaner said his research is "helping evolution," just as millions of years ago humans had fur, but are now naked (Bennet).

- In 1994, a researcher at an international symposium on the artificial insemination of poultry joked that his talk, "Beyond Freezing Semen," should be called "The Night of the Living Dead." Asked what he did with the bird chimeras—birds with genes from other species inserted into their embryos—who hatch with no outward sign of the desired change, he said, "We simply throw them away" (Etches).

From the laboratory, "industrialized" chickens go from being embryonated in eggs in filthy factory hatcheries and breeding facilities to being locked up in dirty dark sheds. They are buried in a rhetoric of exploitation equivalent to the layers of material coverup in which their "silent" suffering goes on. The purpose of a "broiler" chicken is to be buried in the gastrointestinal tract of a human being. The egg, once a symbol of life, is now the symbol of a tomb.

Like the existence of prisoners in the Nazi concentration camps, the existence of chickens in the poultry industry is marked by a ceaseless interplay between forced labor and extermination, between existence as bodily "performance" and existence as industrial waste. Chickens showing poor performance are culled in front of their peers. They are stuffed dead and alive in trash cans in the chicken houses and tossed in piles outside the door in the dirt. Hens deemed no longer fit for commercial egg production are trucked to slaughterhouses, gassed, or buried alive in dumpsters and landfills after being entombed in metal cages inside the walls of windowless buildings. When the manure pits are bulldozed at the end of a laying cycle, hens still stuck in the manure are scooped up with the waste and buried alive on the trucks (Mark, 25–26; Stanley-Branscum).

In *The New Yorker*, Michael Specter describes his visit to the Eastern Shore of the United States to investigate broiler chicken farms. Here is an example of what he found:

Except for the low hum of a ventilation system, the sheds that I approached were quiet. Every window was covered with thick blackout curtains, and it seemed as if nothing at all were inside. After a few stops without finding a farmer at home, I decided to try one of the doors. It wasn't locked, so I unfastened the latch, swung it open, and walked inside. I was almost knocked to the ground by the overpowering smell of feces and ammonia. My eyes burned and so did my lungs, and I could neither see nor breathe. I put my arm across my mouth and immediately moved back toward the door, where I saw a dimmer switch. I turned it up.

There must have been thirty thousand chickens sitting silently on the floor in front of me. They didn't move, didn't cluck. They were almost like statues of chickens, living in nearly total darkness, and they would spend every minute of their six-week lives that way. Despite the ventilation system, there wasn't much air in the room, and I fled quickly. I drove down Route 13, past trailer homes and one-room shacks, each of which seemed to have a dog chained to a stake in the ground. Eventually, I came across a nice-looking farm, with a couple of big chicken sheds. There was a slightly incongruous sign out front that said "Marshall's Seafood." Phillip Marshall was sitting on his Bobcat cleaning out a chicken shed—a crop had just been taken to market. On top of the dirt pile, about to be dropped into a Dumpster, a six-week-old chicken was writhing, its head mangled and its bones visibly crushed. But its vastly oversized chest was heaving up and down and its beak dug slowly into the dirt. After a few minutes, Marshall dumped the load and I introduced myself (Specter, 63).

To conceive of a world such as this, in which indifference to animal suffering is as normal as apple pie, is to understand something of how the Nazis could have "happened" in Germany, how, at Birkenau for example, with similar impassiveness, people could watch their human victims being gassed to death ("Gestapo men stood in a position which enabled them to watch in gas masks the death of the masses of victims"), load the corpses (perhaps not all of them corpses yet) and take them outside Auschwitz "by means of huge shovels," bury the lot, and return for the next batch (Breitman, 118).

Like the rise of animal factories out of traditional farming practices in the twentieth century, the Holocaust of the twentieth century arose as an unprecedented event, yet also as one deeply rooted in age-old attitudes and practices of cruelty and abuse. And just as both events may be seen, in part, as outgrowths of the depression of the 1930s—as government responses to the devastated national economies that prevailed between World War One and World War Two, brought on by the governments themselves—so both may be seen in part as expressions of the Western mania for mechanization and industrial technology extended into virtually every sphere of life, from the Chicago stockyards to Ford motor cars to Auschwitz, and beyond.

Chapter Six

SCAPEGOATS AND SURROGATES: FALSIFYING THE FATE OF VICTIMS

By calling the victims of the Nazis "martyrs," we falsify their fate. The true meaning of "martyr" is: "one who voluntarily undergoes the penalty of death for refusing to renounce his faith." . . . Millions of Jews were systematically slaughtered, as were untold other "undesirables," not for any convictions of theirs, but only because they stood in the way of the realization of an illusion. They neither died for their convictions, nor were they slaughtered because of their convictions, but only in consequence of the Nazis' delusional belief about what was required to protect the purity of their assumed superior racial endowment, and what they thought necessary to guarantee them the living space they believed they needed and were entitled to. Thus while these millions were slaughtered for an idea, they did not die for one.—**Bruno Bettelheim**, "The Holocaust—One Generation Later"

Hasidic literature describes how animals and birds gather of their own accord around a certain ritual slaughterer. Why? Because they realize that their human souls will be liberated when he slaughters them.—**Elijah Judah Schochet**, *Animal Life in Jewish Tradition*

> *When, therefore, the hour demanded the sacrifice, the ox lowed, and swam over the sea, and the guards of the city opened the gates to it. Then the ox directly ran into the city, and stood at the altar, and was sacrificed to the Goddess. Not unreasonably, therefore, was it thought to be most pious to sacrifice many animals, since it appeared that the sacrifice of them was pleasing to the Gods.*—**Porphyry**, *On Abstinence from Animal Food*

> *. . . ideological camouflages for self-serving practices . . .*
> —**Peter Singer**, *Animal Liberation*

Above all, animal factories and the Holocaust share a common denominator of victimization of individuals and groups regarded by those in power as worthless, or "unworthy of life," except in the realm of instrumentality, where, by contrast, they are assigned a role of principal importance. There, whatever is done to them is said to be "justified" by the victims themselves, by virtue of who and what they are. Only by being sacrificed to the "higher" forms of life can these "lower and degraded" forms be redeemed from being, as it were, "just animals." However at variance with outward appearance, the victims are represented as collaborating, at the level of their destiny, if under no other determinable aspect, in their own destruction.

The idea that some groups were "made" to serve others— that they are on the earth to suffer and die sacrificially for a superior group and that group's deity—goes far back in time. The idea is deeply embedded in the culture of the West, which is rooted in ancient Greek and Hebrew modes of thought, and incorporated in Christianity where these roots combine. Details vary, but the essential doctrine holds that the world is arranged in a hierarchy of forms ranging from lowest to highest—from matter to spirit, imperfection to perfection, dust to deity. Most importantly, the world thus conceived represents a moral hierarchy of value, duties, and rights ascending from the "least worthy" forms of existence up to the highest and "most worthy" personages. Within this scheme, some individuals and classes have souls, others do not; some have reason, others do not; some were made in God's image, others were not; some are servants and slaves by nature; others are by nature rulers and gods.

The ancient Greek philosopher Aristotle representatively and influentially "thought that some men are slaves by nature and that slavery is both right and expedient for them" (Singer 1990, 188). Philosopher Peter Singer summarizes Aristotle's outlook in his book *Animal Liberation*. In the chapter "Man's Dominion," he writes: "For Aristotle the man who is by nature a slave is undoubtedly a human being, and is as capable of feeling pleasure and pain as any other human being; yet because he is supposed to be inferior to the free man in his reasoning powers, Aristotle regards him as a 'living instrument' [who,] 'though remaining a human being, is also an article of property'" (1990, 189).

"Man" for Aristotle was part of a scheme of nature, conceived as "essentially a hierarchy in which those with less reasoning ability exist for the sake of those with more":

> Plants exist for the sake of animals, and brute beasts for the sake of man—domestic animals for his use and food, wild ones (or at any rate most of them) for food and other accessories of life, such as clothing and various tools (Aristotle quoted in Singer 1990, 189).

In this wowrldview, "the imperfect is for the sake of the perfect, the irrational is to serve the rational" (Singer 1990, 196), and the "innocent" is charged with bearing the burden of the guilty, even though the "innocent" one is often regarded merely as a vehicle or receptacle for the corruption of the guilty. Of animals sacrificed in biblical rituals, Elijah Judah Schochet writes:

> Now at times a certain aura or mystique does seem to surround certain scriptural animals, notably those involved in several dramatic ritual-purification ceremonies. However, upon closer examination, these animals prove to be not the *source* of cleansing or purification, but rather merely the *vehicle* for the achievement of this desirable state. [For example], Leviticus describes the selection of two he-goats, one designated for God, on for Azazel. The former was sacrificed "to make atonement," while the latter was driven off into the wilderness. It may be tempting to view the scapegoat as a surrogate or substitute for the life of the human being who has transgressed, but more accurately, the animal is merely the vehicle for the removal and disposal of the taint of transgression. The significance of the ceremony is not the goat itself, but rather the transgressions that it bears off into the wilderness (Schochet, 30).

Silence of the Lambs

In *Animals in the Third Reich*, Boria Sax writes: "Uncertain on its feet and constantly calling for its mother, the lamb is a symbol of helplessness, passivity, and innocence" (56). The symbol of the lamb in the Old Testament is rooted in the pastoral economy of the Hebrews. Lambs were part of the landscape and culture, and as Sax writes, "there was a special intimacy between sheep and human beings in the Old Testament" (56).

In the New Testament, by contrast, lambs essentially disappear from the symbol they inspired. In Christianity, lambs are anthropomorphized in the original sense of ascribing human attributes to a deity. God, in Christianity, becomes Man in the form of his Son, Jesus. As Carol J. Adams and Marjorie Procter-Smith write, "When Christians use lamb language, they are not talking about lambs, they are not thinking about lambs, they are thinking about Jesus" (307–308).

The passivity of sheep and lambs in being led to slaughter suggested how Jesus, when arrested in Gethsemene, did not fight back and ordered his followers not to retaliate. Like the sacrificial lamb believed to anticipate his sacrifice, Jesus was "led as a sheep to the slaughter" (Acts 8:32). On seeing Jesus for the first time, John the Baptist said, "Behold the Lamb of God, who takes away the sin of the world" (John 1:29).

In "Taking Life or 'Taking on Life'?" Carol J. Adams and Marjorie Procter-Smith write concerning the disappearance of the lamb in Christianity: "As the lamb becomes appropriated into metaphor for Jesus' sacrifice, the reality of the suffering of individual lambs who are slaughtered for food is forgotten. The lambs are rendered appropriate victims at the same time that their victimization disappears. . . . The lamb in Christian communion becomes doubly removed, first by being slaughtered and then by being resymbolized as a human male" (307).

Christian theologian Andrew Linzey laments the fact that Christianity offers few opportunities to celebrate the life of animals, and that Christians "go on worshipping as though the world of animals was invisible" (Linzey, 23). Lambs exemplify and symbolize this invisibility. In Christianity, the sacrifice of Jesus was believed to render animal sacrifice superfluous. According to St. Paul, Christians "are sanctified through the offering of the body of Jesus Christ once for all" (Hebrews 10:10), whereas "it is not possible that the blood of bulls and of goats should take away sins" (Hebrews 10:4), because animal blood is of the flesh and not the spirit.

Denied spiritual significance, animals had no further place in the Christian doctrine of salvation. "The sacraments of Christianity," Boria Sax writes, "all center either, like marriage, around the relations between human beings or, like communion, around the relation of a person to God. There is almost nothing in Christian ritual that regulates or sanctifies relationships between human beings and other creatures" (142). In 1 Corinthians 9:9–10, St. Paul asks regarding the Mosaic law forbidding muzzling the ox that treads out the corn, "Does God take care for oxen? Or does he say this altogether for our sakes? For our sakes no doubt," he concludes.

"Flickers of Concern"

Eager to get people to care about animals and their suffering, animal rights advocates have sought to show that the Bible does include an ethical concern for animals, as indicated in the above-cited Mosaic instruction, in Deuteronomy 25:4, to refrain from muzzling an ox while he is threshing. According to Norm Phelps in his book *The Dominion of Love: Animal Rights According to the Bible*, "This presumes that the ox can experience both the physical distress of hunger and the emotional distress of being tantalized by food that he cannot have" (Phelps, 180). This is a reasonable interpretation, and it is certainly important to draw people's attention to Bible verses that show compassion for animals and encourage consideration of their feelings.

However, as Peter Singer writes concerning the Old Testament, the Bible shows, at most, "flickers of concern for [animals'] suffering" (Singer 1990, 191). As for the New Testament, he says it is "completely lacking in any injunction against cruelty to animals, or any recommendation to consider their interests. Jesus himself is described as showing apparent indifference to the fate of nonhumans when he induced two thousand swine to hurl themselves into the sea—an act which was apparently quite unnecessary, since Jesus was well able to cast out devils without inflicting them upon any other creature" (Singer 1990, 191).

Jewish writers in the animal rights movement have been quick to emphasize those "flickers of concern"—the potential in Judaism to evolve an ethic of compassion for nonhuman animals. In his book *Judaism and Vegetarianism*, Richard Schwartz writes that the Jewish tradition "clearly indicates that we are forbidden to be cruel to animals and that we are to treat them with compassion. These concepts are summarized in the Hebrew phrase *tsa' ar ba' alei chayim*, the biblical mandate not to cause 'pain to any living creature' (Schwartz, 15).[4] Similarly, in *Rabbis and Vegetarianism: An Evolving Tradition*, Roberta Kalechofsky writes that a "quiet revolution is taking place in the millennial tradition of kashruth [Jewish dietary practices], whose vegetarian sentiment has been fermenting throughout Jewish history":

> The "provegetarian bias" was recognized and explored throughout the centuries of the Nazaritic tradition, Kabbalistic mystics, Essenes, and the Karaites who banned meat-eating in the tenth century (but, alas! became backsliders). By the late nineteenth and early twentieth centuries, the "provegetarian bias" became a prominent theme, as evidenced by the writings of Rabbi Medini, Rev. Chaim Maccoby, and Rav Kook. More contemporarily, a confluence of reasons based on revulsion toward modern husbandry, the Holocaust, and the felt need to move away from all expressions of violence, motivate the Jewish vegetarian movement (Kalechofsky 1995, ii).

Writers who perceive a strain of ethical concern for animals in the Bible remind us that the Garden of Eden was vegetarian and nonviolent, and that Noah's permission to eat meat after the Flood was God's concession to humanity's moral degeneration: "And God looked upon the earth, and, behold, it was corrupt; for all flesh had corrupted their way upon the earth" (Genesis 6:12). They draw attention to the Bible's occasional, albeit powerful, images of a restored Eden or peaceable kingdom where they "shall not hurt nor destroy in all my holy mountain; for the earth shall be full of the knowledge of the Lord" (Isaiah 11:9). Also noted is the condemnation of animal sacrifice by the eighth century BCE prophets, beginning with the prophet Isaiah, and proceeding through Jeremiah, Hosea, Amos, and Micah. According to J. R. Hyland, in *God's Covenant with Animals*, their prophecies "reiterated that the sacrifice of animals was an abomination in the sight of God, an unholy practice that demanded repentance" (Hyland, 8).

Isaiah upbraided Israel:

To what purpose is the multitude of your sacrifices unto me? says the Lord: I am full of the burnt offerings of rams, and the fat of fed beasts; and I delight not in the blood of bullocks, or of lambs, or of he goats (Isaiah 1:11).

Speaking for God, Amos thundered to the errant tribes:

I hate, I despise your feast days, and I will not smell in your solemn assemblies. Though you offer me burnt offerings and your meat offerings, I will not accept them: neither will I regard the peace offerings of your fat beasts (Amos 5:21–22).

And Jeremiah declared, ambiguously:

Thus says the Lord of hosts, the God of Israel; Put your burnt offerings unto your sacrifices, and eat flesh. For I spoke not unto your fathers, nor commanded them in the day that I brought them out of the land of Egypt, concerning burnt offerings or sacrifices: But this thing I commanded them, saying, Obey my voice, and I will be

your God and you shall be my people (Jeremiah
7:21–23).

Reading these words in context, it is not clear how far the
prophets were moved by compassion for the sacrificed animals. They condemn stealing, murder, adultery, swearing false-
ly, burning incense to local fertility gods (Baalim), and chasing
after strange gods (Jeremiah 7:9–10). Condemnation of animal
sacrifice seems mainly directed against the attempt to substitute formalistic offerings in lieu of genuine religious conduct
and obedience to Yahweh. God rejects burnt offerings, but he
also rejects incense and sugarcane offered in a spirit of false
piety. By the same token, in Jeremiah 7:6, Israel is urged to
"shed not innocent blood in this place," thus placing animal
sacrifice together with oppressing the stranger, the fatherless,
and the widow—assuming that the "innocent blood" is, or
includes, that of nonhuman beings:

> If you oppress not the stranger, the fatherless, and the
> widow, and shed not innocent blood in this place, nei-
> ther walk after other gods to your hurt: Then I will cause
> you to dwell in this place, in the land that I gave to your
> fathers, forever and ever (Jeremiah 7:6–7).

"Kill the Passover"—Exodus 12:21

However, Jeremiah's claim that God did not command burnt
offerings or sacrifices when he delivered Israel from Egypt does
not fit the story told in Exodus. In Exodus 12:12, when God
decides to kill all the firstborn in Egypt, "both man and beast,"
but spare the Hebrews, he gives Moses explicit instructions for
raising, killing, roasting, and eating lambs whose blood is to be
smeared over the door of each father's household signaling to
God to pass over those houses on his rampage. On the tenth

day of the month, each house is to take an unblemished lamb from the sheep or goats (Exodus 12:3–5).

> And you shall keep it up until the fourteenth day of the same month; and the whole assembly of the congregation of Israel shall kill it in the evening. And they shall take of the blood and strike it on the two side posts and on the upper door post of the houses, wherein they shall eat it. And they shall eat the flesh in that night, roast with fire. . . . Eat not of it raw, nor sodden at all with water, but roast it with fire; his head with his legs. . . . And you shall let nothing of it remain until the morning; and that which remains of it until the morning you shall burn with fire. . . . For I will pass through the land of Egypt this night, and will smite all the first-born in the land of Egypt, both man and beast; and against all the gods of Egypt I will execute judgment. . . . And the blood shall be to you a token upon the houses where you are: and when I see the blood, I will pass over you, and the plague shall not be upon you to destroy you, when I smite the land of Egypt. And this day shall be unto you for a memorial; and you shall keep it a feast to the Lord throughout your generations; you shall keep it a feast by ordinance forever (Exodus 12: 6–14).

Three months later, after their deliverance from Egypt, the people of Israel are ordered by God, speaking through Moses in the wilderness, to make an altar and "sacrifice thereon your burnt offerings, and your peace offerings, your sheep, and your oxen" (Exodus 20:24). In Exodus 24:4–8, Moses builds the altar and sprinkles on it, and on the congregation, the blood of "burnt offerings, and sacrificed peace offerings of oxen." Further on, God tells Moses, concerning the building of the tabernacle: "And you shall set the altar of the burnt offering before the door to the tabernacle of the tent of the congregation. . . . And you shall anoint the altar of the burnt offering" (Exodus 40:6, 10). In verse 29, Moses is said to have "put the altar of burnt offering by the door of the tabernacle of the tent of the congregation, and offered upon it the burnt offering and the meat offering; as the Lord commanded Moses."

Animals in the Bible

In *Animal Life in Jewish Tradition: Attitudes and Relationships*, Elijah Judah Schochet rejects any interpretation that would place nonhumans on a level with humans or regard the mistreatment of animals as sinful. "The concern of the prophets," he writes, "was exclusively with man's relationship to his fellow-man, not his conduct toward beasts" (Schochet, 74).

> Repeatedly, the poor, the widow, the orphan, and the stranger are singled out as the defenseless classes, deserving of special compassion, and those who mistreat them are vigorously condemned. But no similar condemnation is leveled against those who mistreat helpless animals (Schochet, 74).

As for the prophets' condemnation of animal sacrifice, Schochet argues that this has "nothing at all to do with any feelings of compassion for the sacrificial animal":

> Nor, indeed, do the prophets object to sacrifice per se, for Isaiah is also critical of prayer that is bereft of the proper ethical commitment. What concerned the prophets was that any rite, minus right, is wrong; that sacrifices unaccompanied by corresponding ethical behavior were empty gestures. They demanded moral obedience along with ritual devotions, but nowhere in

Scripture is there the slightest objection to animal sacrifices on ethical grounds (Schochet, 75).

While the ancient Hebrew might have felt compassion for
his animals, this was not, says Schochet, "a central or serious
concern in his life" (75), and nowhere in the Bible is it implied,
he argues, "that animals deserve, *in their own right*, to be treated compassionately" (76). In situations where kindness to animals is shown, "the point," he says, "is not kindness to the animal per se." Rather, kindness to animals is regarded as an indi-
cator of behavior towards people. And it is simply good sense
not to mistreat your property. In the Bible, the animal, according to Schochet, is "akin more to a tool than to a slave" (76).

While Schochet places the ancient Hebrew view of animals
and nature above that of the pagan, they agreed, he insists,
despite other differences, that animals did not merit attention
or concern in their own right:

In summary, for most ancients, fauna were objects of
worship, endowed with prescience, sanctity, and
demonic powers. It was therefore not unusual for these
creatures to be venerated and worshipped. But the animal kingdom, as a whole, did not merit attention or
concern. In contrast, the religion of Israel dedeified
fauna. There was no reverence, and certainly no worship of the beast, but neither was the beast mistreated.
As God's most delicate tool, animals were entitled to
rights and protection (Schochet, 78–79).

However, God's "animal tools" *are* mistreated in the Bible,
and so are humans. In the Bible, God repeatedly punishes and
threatens to punish everything and everyone for the transgressions of a few people. For example, in Jeremiah 7:21, God tells
Israel: "Behold, mine anger and my fury shall be poured out

upon this place, upon man, and upon beast, and upon the trees of the field, and upon the fruit of the ground; and it shall burn, and shall not be quenched."

If the Bible is a sacred text with themes of compassion, it is also an epic drama filled with retaliatory mass murders and sacrificial bloodshed. Animals are made to suffer for human sins,[5] and the blood sacrifice of Jesus, the "Lamb of God," is the starting point of Christianity. As for Israel, J. R. Hyland writes that for 500 years after Jerusalem fell to the Babylonians in 587 BCE, "the Jewish people slaughtered, or were themselves slaughtered, in the endless power struggles that centered on Palestine. The blood of sacrificial victims ran deep in the House of God while the blood of war victims ran deep in the streets beyond the Temple walls. . . . Finally the Jewish people became embroiled in a brutal civil war in which Pharisee and Sadducee tortured and killed each other as mercilessly as any outsider would have done" (Hyland, 39).

Norm Phelps writes similarly that, far from being an invention of the twentieth century or the exclusive fate of the Jews under the Nazis, genocide and ethnic cleansing were endemic to the ancient world. In Numbers 31, God orders Israel to exterminate the Midianites, and in 1 Samuel, he orders Israel to kill the Amalekite king, Agag, and all he has, "both man and woman, infant and suckling, ox and sheep, camel and ass" (1 Samuel 15:3). These are not isolated incidents. Rather, Phelps points out that there are "at least ten other occasions on which we are told that the Israelites, presumably in obedience to God's command, exterminated in cold blood the entire civilian populations of towns or tribes whom they had defeated in battle" (Phelps, 14–15).

As human warfare raged, animals were slaughtered in the temples. Along with "the wars and assassinations, pestilence and famine, bloodshed and exile described in the Bible," there were, as Isaac Bashevis Singer ruefully observes, "the sacrifices the priests used to burn on the altar: the sheep, the rams, the goats, and the doves whose heads they wrung off and whose blood they sprung as a sweet savor unto the Lord" (Patterson, 171).

Fictions of Reciprocity

In "Taking Life or 'Taking On Life'?" Carol J. Adams and Marjorie Procter-Smith cite the following anecdote from the nineteenth-century women's movement:

> When Pundita Ramabia was in this country she saw a hen carried to market with its [sic] head downward. This Christian method of treating a poor, dumb creature caused the heathen woman to cry out, "Oh, how cruel to carry a hen with its head down!" and she quickly received the reply, "Why, the hen does not mind it"; and in her heathen innocence she inquired, "Did you ask the hen?" (302)

Similar to the myths circulated by US slavery owners about their human "property" during the nineteenth century, animal victimizers typically insist that their victims don't mind their plight, or that they don't experience it "as you or I would," or that the victims are complicit in their plight, even, on occasion, to the point of gratitude. The victims, in other words, are not really "innocent." Thus, for example, at his trial, Nazi leader Adolf Eichmann pleaded, regarding his deportation of tens of thousands of Jews to their deaths, that the Jews "desired" to emigrate and that "he, Eichmann, was there to help them" (Arendt 1964, 48). This is not exceptional psychology, as students of sexual assault are well aware. Indeed, victimizers are very often likely to represent themselves, and to be upheld by their sympathizers, as the innocent parties in their orchestrations of the suffering and death of others. In *Eichmann in Jerusalem*, Hannah Arendt cites an Egyptian deputy foreign minister who claimed, for instance, that Hitler was "innocent of the slaughter of the Jews; he was a victim of the Zionists, who had 'compelled him to perpetrate crimes that would eventually enable them to achieve their aim—the creation of the State of Israel'" (Arendt 1964, 20). If you want to hurt someone and maintain a clean conscience about it, chances are you will invoke arguments along one or more of these lines: the slave/animal doesn't feel, doesn't know, doesn't care, is complicit, or isn't even *there*. In the latter case the victim is configured as *an illusion*.

This is a commonplace of victimizer psychology: the transformation of the sacrificial victim into a manifestation of something else in disguise, a being or spirit imprisoned in the manifestation that wants to be "let out," a "vermin" or viral infection that requires a bloodletting ceremony of purgation to protect the community, "race," or nation. In such cases, not only is the victim reconfigured to suit the victimizer's agenda, but the victimizer too is different from what he or she appears to be—a murderer, say, as in the portrayal of Hitler as, "in reality," the benignly motivated liberator of a spiritual wish within the Jewish people to be free (think also of US president George W. Bush as the alleged "liberator" of the Iraqi people).

To this day, animals are ritually sacrificed by Hindus whose practice is based on the idea that "the sacrifice of an animal is *not really the killing of an animal*." The animal to be sacrificed "is not considered an animal" but is instead "a symbol of those powers for which the sacrificial ritual stands" (Lal 1986, 201).

In Hindu mythology, according to Basant K. Lal, "if a soul migrates to an animal form from a human life, it moves from a superior to an inferior form of life, and it does so because of its misdeeds while in the human form" (Lal, 206). As in traditional Judaism, the Hindu attitude toward animals "is based *not* on considerations about the *animal* as such but on considerations about how the development of this attitude is a part of the purificatory steps" to human salvation (Lal, 200). Similarly in Buddhism, according to Christopher Chapple, the animal world is one of the lesser destinies, "along with the hell beings and hungry ghosts." Birth as an animal, he writes, "is said to be punishment for evil deeds." Particularly "through deludedness one becomes an animal" (Chapple, 219).

Indeed, there is a long tradition of thought in ancient Greek religion, in Judaic mysticism, and in other sectors of human culture in which nonhumans are said to benefit from being sacrificed by humans to the point of voluntarily "stretching out their necks" to assist in being slaughtered (Porphyry 1965, 36–37; Schochet 1984, 236–244; Schwartz 2001, 124–127). As Schochet says about the doctrine of metempsychosis (the belief that human souls can become trapped in "lower" life forms as punishment for their misdeeds), this doctrine, rather than promoting vegetarianism, "militated in favor of the consumption of flesh, for one thereby did the animal a favor" in releasing the human soul within to pursue its higher destiny (Schochet, 244). He tells the story of a calf brought into the city to be slaughtered. When the calf sheds tears, the slaughterer interprets the calf as a "transmigrated" dead man whose sinful soul needed improvement. Prepared for slaughter, the calf "willing stretches out its neck beneath the slaughterer's knife." The slaughterer kills the calf and eats him. The following night he dreams that the liberated dead man thanks him for slaughtering the calf—"Blessed are you for having given peace to my soul" (Schochet, 243).

In Isaac Bashevis Singer's short story "The Slaughterer," the rabbi seeks to convince the main character, Yoineh Meir, who does not want to slaughter animals for a living but is coerced into doing so, that by slaughtering animals for people to eat, he frees imprisoned souls:

When you slaughter an animal with a pure knife and with piety, you liberate the soul that resides in it. For it is well known that the souls of saints often transmigrate into the bodies of cows, fowl, and fish to do penance for some offence (Singer 1982, 207).

In *Judaism and Vegetarianism*, Richard Schwartz says that many stories are told about the early Chassidic masters [Jewish mystics in Eastern Europe in the Middle Ages and beyond] in which "the soul in the animal asks the Rebbe [Rabbi] to consume its meat and use the resultant strength for a specific *mitzvah* [commandment], in order to offset the sin and set the soul free to reincarnate as a human being once again" (Schwartz, 124). He cites, for example, a nineteenth-century tale that features a Chassidic Rabbi "so pure and holy" that "flocks of wild doves came of their own accord to lie down under his knife." The "thousands of poor human souls reincarnated" in these doves, this "kosher species of animals," begged to be liberated from their degraded embodiment as doves (Schwartz, 125).

Little has changed since earlier times. In today's world, advertisers tell us that pigs want to become Oscar Mayer wieners; they represent "fast-food" chickens fighting to be the tastiest chicken sandwich (HSUS). In the sacrificial language of Western science, animals who are but "tools of research" under one aspect stand forth as "engaged" in animal experimentation (Paul-Murphy, et al.).

Regardless of what else is involved, the slaughter of an animal is typically represented as merely "incidental" in the process of fulfilling a particular human purpose, whether it be connecting with God, enjoying the outdoors, or uniting family members. In such cases, the animals "are rendered appropriate victims at the same time that their victimization disappears" (Adams and Procter-Smith, 307).[6] Regarding religious sacrifice, Godfrey Ashby argues:

It is perhaps best to avoid the technical term "victim," since this has acquired emotive overtones which are usually absent from sacrifices. . . . It is essential to appreciate that, even in human sacrifice, the death of the living creature is not seen as a tragedy, any more than the death of a sheep is today seen as a tragedy before roast mutton. . . . [The] death is incidental (Adams and Procter-Smith, 306–307).

Writing in the nineteenth century, William Howitt defends sport hunting against charges of cruelty as follows:

The pleasure is in the pursuit of an object, and the art and activity by which a wild creature is captured, and in all those concomitants of pleasant scenery and pleasant seasons that enter into the enjoyment of rural sports;— the suffering is only the casual adjunct . . . the momentary pang of a creature, which forms but one atom in a living series (Howitt, 47).

And Ellen Goodman writes in *The Washington Post* that even though the consumption of animal products is essential to her family's enjoyment of Thanksgiving, it isn't "really" the turkey, the chicken fat, and the eggs that she gushes over in her column, "The Seasonal Equivalent of Quality Time" (31A). Rather, "it is really our appetite for togetherness that will bring us to the Thanksgiving table." Presumably she would say that the animals who suffer and die for these dinners are merely the "casual adjuncts" of the family gathering.

Challenging the Rhetoric of Exploitation
Challenges such as PETA's "Holocaust on Your Plate" exhibit and Charles Patterson's book *Eternal Treblinka: Our Treatment of*

Animals and the Holocaust help to restore the animals' point of view amid the rhetoric of exploitation. They seek to restore to a piece of meat the sight of "the sad, tortured face that was attached to it some time in the past" (Butler and Alexander, 4). They stimulate people to confront how animals must feel being torn from their mothers, mutilated, burned, imprisoned, and brutally murdered. They force us to recognize that these animals, powerless to defend themselves, are condemned to the same degradation, loneliness, pain, and terror of imprisonment and slaughter as were the Jews, Gypsies, homosexuals, and others characterized as worthless under the Nazis. They flout the taboos and expose the rationalizations. They puncture the solipsism within which we hide, in order to rescue billions of unacknowledged animal victims from the anonymity and injustice of being consigned to the fate of a false and inferior existence in our minds.

The Absent Referent

The holocausts—burnt offerings—of the ancient Hebrews consisted of countless nonhuman animals, as did the religious animal sacrifices conducted throughout the ancient world by the Greeks, Hindus, Muslims, Native Americans, and other cultures (Regan 1986; Davis 2001, 33–43). Yet we are not supposed to regard those animals or their counterparts in today's world, where the consumption of animals for food rises to ever-greater levels—over ten billion animals each year in the United States alone (UPC 2004a). We are not supposed to contemplate the experience of animals in being turned into "burnt offerings," meat, metaphors, and other forms that obliterate their lives, personalities, feelings, and identities that we choose to confer.

The "Holocaust on Your Plate" exhibit restores what feminist writer Carol J. Adams refers to in *The Sexual Politics of Meat* as the "absent referent" (Adams 1990, 40–48). An absent referent is an individual or group whose fate is "transmuted into a metaphor for someone else's existence or fate" without being acknowledged in its own right. According to Adams, "Metaphorically, the absent referent can be anything whose original meaning is undercut as it is absorbed into a different hierarchy of meaning." The rape of women, for example, can be applied metaphorically to the "rape of the earth" in such a way as to obliterate women. Adams explains:

> The absent referent is both there and not there. It is there through inference, but its meaningfulness reflects only upon what it refers to because the originating, literal experience that contributes the meaning is not there. We fail to accord this absent referent its own existence (Adams 1990, 42).

In the role of absent referents, nonhuman animals become metaphors for describing human experience at the same time that "the originating oppression of animals that generates the power of the metaphor" is unacknowledged (Adams 1990, 43), as when people say, "We're treated like animals." The meaning of the animals' fate, for the animals themselves, for each individual him and her, is absorbed into a human-centered hierarchy in which the animals do not count, or even exist, apart from how humans use or have used them. Our use becomes their ontology—"this is what they are"—and their teleology—"this is what they were made for."

"Obscuring the face of the other," as Maxwell Schnurer describes in his essay "At the Gates of Hell," is "vital to the reduction of living beings to objects upon whom atrocities can be heaped" (117). And this process is not species-specific or confined to the Nazi era. Schnurer explains the process of obscuring the face of the other to achieve self-exoneration:

In the case of the Holocaust, it was necessary to sustain a complex infrastructure that enabled each participant to disguise his or her responsibility. In the case of animals, as [Carol] Adams notes, it is essential that the acts of killing, enslaving, and torturing animals be well hidden from sight, so that the consumer only ever sees the finished "product." For both systems of oppression, it is critical that the process be as compartmentalized as possible. The reason to obscure the face of suffering is as obvious as it is hidden—the vision of terrible actions can elicit sympathy and compassion, and often call for remedy (Schnurer, 117).

The remedy lies with us. Even Roberta Kalechofsky declares, despite her opposition to Holocaust comparisons, that "Most suffering today, whether of animals or humans, suffering beyond calculation, whether it is physiological or the ripping apart of a mother and offspring, is at the hands of other humans" (67). It is in this sense of being directly responsible for stupendous mass misery and death on earth that humanity as a whole can, and should, claim ownership of the holocaust.

Chapter Seven

THE 9/11 CONTROVERSY

For many Americans, the worst, most unjust suffering to befall anyone happened on September 11, 2001. Mark Slouka, in his essay "A Year Later" in *Harper's Magazine*, puzzled over "how it was possible for a man's faith to sail over Auschwitz, say, only to founder on the World Trade Center" (37). How was it that so many intelligent people he knew, who had lived through the twentieth century and knew something about history, actually insisted "that everything is different now," as a result of 9/11, as though, Slouka marveled, "only *our* sorrow would weigh in the record"? People who said they'd never be the same again never said that while watching on television or reading in the newspaper about other people's and other nations' calamities. In saying that the world as a result of the 9/11 attack was "different now," they didn't mean that "before the 9/11 attack I was blind, but now I see the suffering that is going on and that has been going on all around me, to which I might be a contributor, God forbid." No, they meant that an incomparable and superior outrage had occurred. It happened to Americans. It happened to them: "Rwanda? Bosnia? Couldn't help but feel sorry for those folks, but let's face it: Rwanda did not have a covenant with God. And Jesus was not a Sarajevan," Slouka spoofed (39).

Following the 9/11 attack, I published a letter (Davis 2001; 2002) that raised such consternation in the mainstream media that it got me on *The Howard Stern Show*. Without seeking to diminish the horror of 9/11, I wrote that the people who died in the attack arguably did not suffer more terrible deaths than animals in slaughterhouses suffer every day. Using chickens as an example, I observed that in addition to the much larger number of innocent chickens who were killed (more than 8.5 billion chickens in the United States in 2001 [UPC 2003]), and the horrible deaths they endured in the slaughter plants that day and every day, one had to account for the misery of their lives leading up to their horrible death, including the terror attack they had suffered several hours or days before they were killed, euphemistically referred to as "chicken catching."

I compared all this to the relatively satisfying lives of the majority of human victims of 9/11 prior to the attack and added that we humans have a plethora of palliatives, ranging from proclaiming ourselves heroes and plotting revenge against our malefactors to the consolation of family and friends and the relief of painkilling drugs and alcoholic beverages. Moreover, whereas human animals have the ability to make some sort of sense of the tragedy, the chickens, in contrast, have no cognitive insulation, no compensation, presumably no comprehension of the causes of their suffering, and thus no psychological relief from their suffering. The fact that intensively raised chickens are forced to live in systems that reflect our dispositions, not theirs, and that these systems are inimical to their basic nature (as revealed by their behavior, physical breakdown, and other indicators), shows that they are suffering in ways that could equal and even exceed anything that we have known.

I wrote my rebuttal in response to comments made by philosopher Peter Singer, who in a review of Joan Dunayer's book *Animal Equality: Language and Liberation* (2001) challenged the contention that we should use equally strong words for human and nonhuman suffering or death. He wrote:

"Reading this suggestion just a few days after the killing of several thousand people at the World Trade Centre, I have to demur. It is not speciesist to think that this event was a greater tragedy than the killing of several million chickens, which no doubt also occurred on September 11, as it occurs on every working day in the United States. There are reasons for thinking that the deaths of beings with family ties as close as those between the people killed at the World Trade Centre and their loved ones are more tragic than the deaths of beings without those ties; and there is more that could be said about the kind of loss that death is to beings who have a high degree of self-awareness, and a vivid sense of their own existence over time" (Singer 2002, 36).

There are reasons for contesting this statement of assumed superiority of the human suffering caused by 9/11 over that of the chickens in slaughterhouses, starting with the fact that it is not lofty "tragedy" that's at issue in the book Singer is challenging, but raw suffering.[7] Moreover, there is evidence that the highly social chicken, who is endowed with a "complex nervous system designed to form a multitude of memories and to make complex decisions" (Rogers 218), has self-awareness and a sense of personal existence over time. Not only have humans broken these birds' ties with their own mothers, families, and the natural world, but who are we to say what bonds chickens living together in the miserable chicken houses may or may not have formed? The chickens at United Poultry Concerns (the sanctuary that I run) form close personal attachments. Even chickens exploiters admit that they do (Davis 1996, 35, 148). The avian cognition specialist Lesley J. Rogers, quoted above, says in her book, *The Development of Brain and Behaviour in the Chicken* that modern studies of birds, including chickens, "throw the fallacies of previous assumptions about the inferiority of avian cognition into sharp relief" (218; Davis 1995/96).[8]

It is altogether reasonable to assume that animals in confinement systems designed to exploit them suffer even more, in certain respects, than do humans who are similarly confined, comparable to the way that a cognitively challenged person might experience dimensions of suffering in being rough-handled, imprisoned, and shouted at that elude individuals capable of conceptualizing the experience. Indeed, one who is capable of conceptualizing one's own suffering may be unable to grasp what it feels like to suffer without being able to conceptualize it, of being in a condition that could add to, rather than reduce, the suffering.[9] It is in this quite different sense from what is usually meant, when we are told that it is "meaningless" to compare the suffering of a chicken with that of a human being, that the claim resonates. Biologist Marian Stamp Dawkins says that other animal species "may suffer in states that no human has ever dreamed of or experienced" (Dawkins, 29). Matthew Scully writes in *Dominion* of the pain and suffering of animals in human confinement systems:

> For all we know, their pain may sometimes seem more immediate, blunt, arbitrary, and inescapable than ours. Walk through an animal shelter or slaughterhouse and you wonder if animal suffering might not at times be all the more terrifying and all-encompassing without benefit of the words and concepts that for us, after all, confer not only meaning but consolation. Whatever's going on inside their heads, it doesn't seem "mere" to them (Scully, 7).

Cognitive Distance from Nonhuman Animal Suffering
But even if it could be proven that chickens and other nonhuman animals suffer less than humans condemned to similar situations, this would not mean that nonhuman animals do not suffer profoundly, nor does it provide justification for

harming them. Scientists tell us, for example, that hens in transport trucks have been shown "to experience a level of fear comparable to that induced by exposure to a high-intensity electric shock" (Mills and Nicol, 212). What more do we need to know? Our cognitive distance from nonhuman animal suffering constitutes neither an argument nor evidence as to who suffers more under horrific circumstances, humans or nonhumans. Even for animal advocates, words like "slaughter," "cages," "debeaking," "forced molting," and "ammonia burn" can lose their edge, causing us to forget that what have become routine matters in our minds—like "the killing of several million chickens that occurs on every single working day in the United States," in Peter Singer's reality-blunting phrase—is a fresh experience for each bird who is forced to endure what these words signify.

In any case, the cognitive distance can be reduced. Vicarious suffering is possible with respect to the members of not just one's own species but also other animal species, to whom we are linked through evolution. As Marian Stamp Dawkins says in her essay, "The Scientific Basis for Assessing Suffering in Animals," just as the lack of absolute certainty does not stop us from making assumptions about feelings in other people, so "it is possible to build up a reasonably convincing picture of what animals experience if the right facts about them are accumulated" (28).

Reams of data aren't necessary. We need only to enlist our basic human intelligence to imagine, for example, how a grazing land animal, such as a sheep, must feel in being forcibly herded onto a huge, ugly ship and freighted from Australia to Saudi Arabia or Iraq, jammed in a filthy pen while floating seasickeningly in the Persian Gulf on the way to being slaughtered (Lane).

In the eighteenth century, the New Jersey Quaker John Woolman noted the despondency of chickens on a boat going from America to England and the poignancy of their hopeful response when they came close to land (Davis 1996, 10). If we cannot imagine what it must be like for a sheep or a cow to be placed in a situation comparable to a human being shoved in a cattle car packed with other terrified people headed towards death, if we cannot imagine how chickens must feel being grabbed by their legs in the middle of the night by men who are cursing and yelling at them while pitching and stuffing them into the crates in which they will travel to the next wave of human terror attacks on them at the slaughterhouse, then perhaps we should try to imagine ourselves placed helplessly in the hands of an overpowering extraterrestrial species, to whom our pleas for mercy sound like nothing more than bleats and squeals and clucks—mere "noise" to the master race in whose "superior" minds we are "only animals."

Chapter Eight

AN ATROCITY CAN BE BOTH UNIQUE AND GENERAL

Hitler declared: "He who does not possess power loses the right to life." Nowhere has this belief found more fertile soil than in modern America, where every day millions of lambs, calves, pigs, chickens, cows, horses, and other animals, most of them very young and all of them innocent, are transported to killing centers to be slaughtered for the tables of the master species. Why? Because they can't fight back and defend themselves against those who would kill and eat them, and because there are so few people willing and able to take up the fight on their behalf. Fortified by denial, indifference, and mindless custom that stretches back to our primitive origins, our society's abuse and exploitation of animals seems hopelessly eternal.
—**Charles Patterson**, *Eternal Treblinka: Our Treatment of Animals and the Holocaust*

Those who can't face a hideous prejudice of our own time, which allows human beings to take all of those they believe to be "less" than ourselves, and use and abuse them, are suffering from the same mindset that allowed Nazis to treat Jews and others in similar ways. Meat eaters are endorsing a system in which people confine and slaughter animals in factory farms comparable to the most notorious concentration camps.
—**Ingrid Newkirk**, *President of People for the Ethical Treatment of Animals*

[T]he garbage dump is crammed with our heads and entrails.
—Rooster narrator of the short story "Cockadoo-dledoo,"
by Isaac Bashevis Singer

Some people will say that treating creatures badly in order to eat them is a far cry from treating creatures badly simply because you hate them, but a key point that Charles Patterson makes in his book *Eternal Treblinka* is that the psychology of contempt for "inferior life" links the Nazi mentality to that which allows us to torture and kill billions of nonhuman animals and millions of human beings with no more concern for them and their suffering than Hannibal Lecter and Jame Gumb feel for their victims, apart from the pleasure they derive from the taste of their victims' pain, in Thomas Harris's book *The Silence of the Lambs*. That book says that the plight of the lambs screaming in the slaughterhouses—the whole human enterprise of degradation, cruelty, and murder—"will not end, ever" (Harris, 366).

Eternal Treblinka reminds us of all those other slaughter-houses that were running alongside the human ones under the Nazis—the "round-the-clock killing and butchering" conduct-ed at Treblinka, Auschwitz, in Dresden, and elsewhere (Patterson, 129). In their diaries and letters, Nazi officials note indifferently such things as "huge slaughter of chickens and pigs" (Patterson, 125), and they dote on their meals. One writes to his wife: "The sight of the dead—including women and children—is not very cheering. Once the cold weather sets in you'll be getting a goose now and again. There are over 200 chattering around here, as well as cows, calves, pigs, hens and turkeys. We live like princes. Today, Sunday, we had roast goose (1/4 each). This evening we are having pigeon" (Patterson, 129).

In *Eternal Treblinka*, chickens and pigs shriek as they are being cursed and butchered. Nazis bare their souls in their letters and diaries. We read the opposing testimony of Holocaust survivors and their descendants. The artist Sue Coe's description of the slaughterhouses she visited are excruciating (Patterson, 65–70). If people can read her account and continue to eat animals, drink their babies' milk and steal their eggs, what hope is there? A question that is raised over and over by those who became vegetarians rather than perpetuate the legacy of butchery in their own lives, is "How can 'we' do to 'them' what was done to 'us' and not even recognize it?" Because, in the words of Albert Kaplan, thus far "we have learned nothing from the Holocaust" (Patterson, 167). Kaplan tells of a visit he made in Israel to a kibbutz Holocaust museum near Haifa: "Around 200 feet from the main entrance to the museum is an Auschwitz for animals from which emanates a horrible odor that envelops the museum. I mentioned it to the museum management. Their reaction was not surprising. 'But they are only chickens'" (Patterson, 166).

Christa Blanke, a former Lutheran pastor in Germany and founder of the organization Animals' Angels, cites a link between how we treat animals and Nazism. First we strip the animals of their dignity—"The degradation of the victim always precedes a murder" (Patterson, 228). But, we want to know, why do humans want to degrade and kill? Serial killer Ted Bundy said that it wasn't that he had no feelings of remorse towards his victims, but that those feelings were weak and ephemeral compared to his rapacious emotions and drives (Rule). Naturalist John Muir wrote that the people he knew enjoyed seeing the passenger pigeons fill the sky, but they liked shooting and eating them more—"Every shotgun was aimed at them" (Teale, 46).

The Holocaust thus raises questions, and we long for answers. Why, in the words of Albert Kaplan, are the majority of Holocaust survivors "no more concerned about animals' suffering than were the Germans concerned about Jews' suffering" (Patterson, 167)? Isaac Bashevis Singer says we pretend animals don't feel in order to justify our cruelty, but why do we want to be cruel to animals? Is comfort with cruelty, taking pleasure in cruelty, a trait that we carry from our past embedded in our genes? Why, when we have the technology to duplicate animal foods with textured vegetable protein, do people continue to insist they have to have meat? Why do we praise technology for developing substitutes for cruder practices in other areas of life while balking at its use to eliminate slaughterhouses, which technology can do? Has Isaac Bashevis Singer's philosophic vegetarianism had any effect on modern mainstream Jewish ideas and lifestyles? And if not, why not? This is not to suggest that the Jewish community should be expected to rise above the rest of humankind, but that the Jewish response raises questions about our species no less than does Nazism.

The Holocaust epitomized an attitude, the manifestation of a base will. It is the attitude that we can do whatever we please, however vicious, if we can get away with it, because "we" are superior and "they," whoever they are, are, so to speak, "just chickens." Paradoxically, therefore, it is possible, indeed it is requisite, to make relevant and enlightening comparisons between the Holocaust and our base treatment of nonhuman animals. We can make comparisons while agreeing with the approach taken by philosopher Brian Luke towards animal abuse. Luke writes: "My opposition to the institutionalized exploitation of animals is not based on a *comparison* between human and animal treatment, but on a consideration of the abuse of animals *in and of itself*" (Luke, 81).

Paradoxically, while the words "Nazi," "Treblinka," and "Holocaust" represent unique historical phenomena, they can also transcend these phenomena to function more broadly. And a broader approach to the Holocaust would appear to hold more promise for a more enlightened and compassionate future, surely, than attempting to privatize the event to the extent that its only permissible reference is self-reference. A broader approach also provides a more just apprehension of past and present atrocities while connecting the Nazis and the Holocaust to the larger ethical challenges confronting humanity.

In *A Little Matter of Genocide: Holocaust and Denial in the Americas 1492 to the Present*, Native American scholar Ward Churchill writes that the experience of the Jews under the Nazis "is unique only in the sense that all such phenomena exhibit unique characteristics. Genocide, as the nazis practiced it, was never something suffered exclusively by the Jews, nor were the nazis singularly guilty of its practice" (Churchill 1997, 35–36). Furthermore, Churchill argues in his Foreword to *Terrorists or Freedom Fighters: Reflections on the Liberation of Animals*: "Given that the key to the 'genocidal mentality' resides, as virtually all commentators agree, in the perpetrators' conscious 'dehumanization of the Other' they have set themselves to exterminating, it follows that removal of the self-assigned license enjoyed by humans to do as they will to/with nonhumans can only serve to better the lot of humans targeted for dehumanization/subjugation/eradication" (Churchill 2004, 2–3).

One of the many questions that emerge from the current debate about the use of the Holocaust to illuminate humankind's relationship to billions of nonhuman animals is the extent to which the outrage of having one's own suffering compared to that of others centers primarily on issues of identity and uniqueness or on issues of superiority and privilege. The ownership of superior and unique suffering has many claimants, but, as Isaac Bashevis Singer observed speaking of chickens, there is no evidence that people are more important than chickens (Shenker, 11).

There is no evidence, either, that human suffering, or

Jewish suffering, is separate from all other suffering, or that it needs to be kept separate and superior in order to maintain its identity. But where, it may be asked, is the evidence that we humans have had enough of inflicting massive preventable suffering on one another and on the individuals of other species, given that we know suffering so well, and claim to abhor it? In *Eternal Treblinka*, Charles Patterson concludes that "the sooner we put an end to our cruel and violent way of life, the better it will be for all of us—perpetrators, bystanders, and victims" (232). Who but the Nazi within us disagrees? If we are going to exterminate someone, let it be the fascist within.

Notes

1. Philosopher Peter Singer's utilitarian outlook includes the view that nonhumans are replaceable entities as long as the balance of pleasure (broadly conceived as overall happiness and well-being) is maintained. See, e.g., the semi-fictional dialogue between "Singer" and his "daughter Naomi" in J.M. Coetzee, *The Lives of Animals*, 85–91. Singer: "If we got another puppy from them [breeders], thus causing one more dog to come into existence, then there would be just as much of all those good aspects of dog-existence." Naomi: "What are you saying—that we could painlessly kill Max [their dog], get another puppy to replace him, and everything would be fine?" (88).

   For a critique of Singer's view that the vast majority of sentient beings are replaceable, see Joan Dunayer, *Speciesism*, pp. 13, 78–79. Indeed, what is the difference between Singer's idea of replaceability and that of exploiters for whom nonhuman animals are replaceable, interchangeable units of production? Farmers speak of "replacement" calves, sows, hens, etc. In William Inge's drama *Splendor in the Grass*, the father tells his son who is grieving for his lost girlfriend that the girlfriend can be replaced by countless other women "just as pretty. Same damn thing."

2. At the same time, a human or nonhuman animal's suffering may be so extreme, so unnatural and unbearable, that the longing arises never to be "seen" again. Take the poem "The Snow Leopard in the MetroToronto Zoo," by Jason Gray:

   He pads on grassy banks behind a fence,
   With measured paces slow and tense.

   Beyond his cage his thoughts are sharp and white;
   he lives a compelled anchorite.

   A solid ghost gone blind with all the green,
   He waits and waits to be unseen (Gray, 56).

3. In fact, however, when the public is exposed to some of the more "dramatic" scenes that are still largely hidden from view—e.g., force-feeding of ducks and geese to produce foie gras, artificial insemination and masturbation of "breeder" turkeys on which the commercial turkey industry is based, treatment of newborn chicks at the hatchery, candid-camera looks at what really goes on inside a slaughterhouse—there is a much greater sense of the individuality of each animal and, one hopes, greater empathy. Undercover video investigations are starting to make this happen—to foreground individual animals in their struggle against their abusers in the midst of the mass suffering in which each animal is submerged in factory-farm settings.

4. Richard Schwartz writes in *Judaism and Vegetarianism*, "This Torah-based teaching is found in all strata of Jewish texts and history and occupies a central place in Jewish ethical practice. It is part of the

Jewish vision of what it means to be a *tzaddik* (righteous individual) and to imitate God's ways. . . . Maimonides and Rabbi Judah ha-Hasid (1150–1217) state that this [teaching] is based on the biblical statement of the angel of God to Balaam, 'Wherefore have you smitten your ass?' (Numbers 22:32). This verse is used in the Talmud as a prime source for its assertion that we are to treat animals humanely" (15, 19).

5. In *Animal Life in Jewish Tradition*, Elijah Judah Schochet offers several likely reasons why nonhuman animals are made to suffer for human sins in Jewish theology: "God provides for his righteous human subjects, while animals, incapable of appreciating his Word, are forced to suffer privation" (21). Animal rape-victims are stoned to death with their human violators because "the animal has come to symbolize the degradation of a human being, and its death may more accurately be viewed as the eradication of a degrading symbol than as the infliction of a punishment per se" (54). Regarding the "culpability of a dumb, passive beast, the answer," Schochet says, "concerns itself solely with a practical dimension, that of the virtue of the human community. Clearly it is more important for the human community to rid itself of a disgusting and shameful reminder than to consider ethical questions involving the punishment of animals" (189). Schochet answers the question posed by Noah's flood—"why should innocent animals suffer because of the corruption of man?"—by paraphrasing the opinion of Alexandrian philosopher Philo Judaeus (20 BCE—40 CE): "all entities were created for the service of human beings, and thus, since human beings were being destroyed, animals might just as well be destroyed too! There simply was no longer any need for an abundance of fauna to serve mankind" (189–190).

6. Is the effort to transform sacrificial victims into something other than they are—to make them "disappear"—a sign of guilt? On the one hand victims are said to be sacrificed to expiate human guilt (e.g., "By sacrificial rites, the gift made to God is accepted, union with God is achieved, and the guilt of man is taken away" [cited in Schochet, 19]). On the other hand, Carol J. Adams and Marjorie Procter-Smith argue that "[w]hether the 'appropriate victim' is a battered woman, an abused child, a political prisoner, or a nonhuman animal destroyed for food or some other purpose, in each case a process of objectification is necessary to protect those who offer the sacrifice from the necessity of feeling guilt" (307).

7. I said further in my rebuttal that from the standpoint of ethical utilitarianism, the 9/11 terrorist attacks arguably reduced the amount of pain and suffering in the world because the majority, if not every single one, of the people who suffered and/or died as a result of the September 11 attack ate, and if they are now alive, continue to eat, chickens, a statement praised in the unfortunately titled "Wolves and Poodles" section of the radical environmental journal *Earth First!* Peter Singer's position regarding the superiority of most human adult suffering and death over the suffering and death of most, if not all, nonhuman beings may be inferred, for example, in his discussion of

damming a river that will adversely affect the nonhuman animals in the area:

> Neither drowning nor starvation is an easy way to die, and the suffering involved in these deaths should . . . be given no less weight than we would give to an equivalent amount of suffering experienced by human beings. . . . But the argument presented above does not require us to regard the death of a nonhuman animal as morally equivalent to the death of a human being, since humans are capable of foresight and forward planning in ways that nonhuman animals are not. This is surely relevant to the seriousness of death, which, in the case of a human being capable of planning for the future, will thwart these plans, and which thus causes a loss that is different in kind from the loss that death causes to beings incapable even of understanding that they exist over time and have a future. It is also entirely legitimate to take into account the greater sense of loss that humans feel when people close to them die; whether nonhuman animals will feel a sense of loss at the death of another animal will depend on the social habits of the species, but in most cases it is unlikely to be as prolonged, and perhaps not as deep, as the grief that humans feel (Singer 2000, 96).

Singer's version of anti-speciesism has so many loopholes that it resembles a piece of animal protective legislation gutted by powerful interest groups including subversion by the legislation's own sponsor. Not only is human supremacy protected, but current evidence showing the complexity of cognition and emotion in other animal species is ignored except in the most patronizing fashion. As to the human presence on earth compared to that of other animals, one shudders to think about what our "plans" have wrought in the past and present and what they bode for the future. However, for Singer and some others in the animal advocacy movement, nonhuman animals are conceived of primarily if not exclusively as containers of suffering and simple pleasures, whereas humans are regarded as so conceptually evolved beyond all other forms of life that, for this reason, humans have not only "interests," which they share with other animals, but also inherent *value*.

How different is this, albeit secular, hierarchical worldview from that of rabbinic Judaism, where "the obvious intellectual gap between man and the animals is a formidable chasm"? According to Schochet, "The activity of supreme importance in rabbinic Judaism was *Talmud Torah*, the study of Torah, an activity obviously limited to the human species alone. Only man can study Torah as a means for the apprehension of God and the attainment of sanctity, as a means of bringing order into a chaotic world and cultivating lives of rational decision-making, as opposed to capriciousness and drift. . . . 'Man, in God's image, has the capacity to reflect and to criticize. All an animal can do is act and respond.' Therefore, the lowliest of humans stands far above the greatest of the animals" (188). For Singer, similarly, the "greatest of the animals," the nonhuman Great Apes, are at best on a par with "intellectually disabled human beings" (Singer 1994, 183).

8. These studies are summarized in a scientific paper presented in *Nature Neuroscience Reviews*, February 2005, Volume 6: "Avian brains and a new understanding of vertebrate brain evolution," by The Avian Brain Nomenclature Consortium. This international group of scientists calls for a new set of words to describe the various parts of a bird's brain as a result of "the now overwhelming evidence . . . that the bulk of a bird's brain is not, as scientists once thought, mere 'basal ganglia'—the part of the brain that simply coordinates instincts. Rather, fully 75 percent of a bird's brain is an intricately wired mass that processes information in much the same way as the vaunted human cerebral cortex" (Weiss).

9. For example, in the case of Superintendent of Belchertown State School v. Saikewicz, a man with an IQ of 10 had leukemia. The court determined that a doctor should not treat him because his lack of intelligence would make the treatment unbearably terrifying. "If he is treated with toxic drugs he will be involuntarily immersed in a state of painful suffering, the reason for which he will never understand. Patients who request treatment know the risks involved and can appreciate the painful side-effects when they arrive. They know the reason for the pain and their hope makes it tolerable" (430). I am grateful to attorney Sean Day for bringing this case to my attention.

References and Bibliography

Adams, Carol. J. 1990. *The Sexual Politics of Meat: A Feminist-Vegetarian Critical Theory*. New York: Continuum.

_____. 1996. "Caring about Suffering: A Feminist Exploration." *Beyond Animal Rights: A Feminist Caring Ethic for the Treatment of Animals*. Ed. Josephine Donovan and Carol J. Adams. New York: Continuum. 170–196.

_____. 2003. *The Pornography of Meat*. New York: Continuum.

Adams, Carol J., and Marjorie Procter-Smith. 1994. "Taking Life or 'Taking on Life'?" *Ecofeminism and the Sacred*. Ed. Carol J. Adams. New York: Continuum.

Alvarez, A. 1999. *Where Did It All Go Right?: A Memoir*. New York: William Morrow.

AP (Associated Press). 2004. "World Photos." 6 February.

Applebaum, Anne. 2003. *Gulag: A History*. New York: Doubleday.

Arendt, Hannah. 1964. *Eichmann in Jerusalem: A Report on the Banality of Evil*. New York: Penguin Books. (This edition published in 1994.)

_____. 2003. "Thinking Through the Good Life." *The Many Faces of Philosophy: Reflections from Plato to Arendt*. Ed. Amelie Oksenberg Rorty. Oxford: Oxford University Press. 472–481.

Atwood. Margaret. 1986. *The Handmaid's Tale*. New York: Anchor Books.

[The] Avian Brain Nomenclature Consortium. 2005. "Avian Brains and a New Understanding of Vertebrate Brain Evolution." *Nature Neuroscience Reviews* Vol. 6 (February): 151–159. Avianbrain.org.

Barad, Judith. 2004. "Aquinas's Account of Anger Applied to the ALF." *Terrorists or Freedom Fighters: Reflections on the Liberation of Animals*. Ed. Steven Best and Anthony J. Nocella II. New York: Lantern Books.

Barnes, Donald J. 1985. "A Matter of Change." *In Defense of Animals*. Ed. Peter Singer. New York: Basil Blackwell. 157–167.

Baskin, Cathryn. 1978. "Confessions of a Chicken Farmer." *Country Journal* April: 37–41. Cited in Davis 1996, 83.

Beirne, Piers. 1997. "Rethinking Bestiality: Towards a Concept of Interspecies Sexual Assault." *Theoretical Criminology* Vol. 1, No. 3: 317–340.

Bell, Donald D., and William D. Weaver, Jr., eds. 2002. *Chicken Meat and Egg Production*, 5th ed. Norwell, Mass: Kluwer Academic Publishers.

Bennet, James. 2002. "Cluck! Cluck! Chickens in Their Birthday Suits!" *New York Times* 24 May: International.

Berger, John. 1985. "Why Look at Animals?" *The Language of the Birds: Tales, Texts, & Poems of Interspecies Communication*. Ed. David M. Guss. San Francisco: North Point Press. 275–287.

Best, Steven, and Anthony J. Nocella II, eds. 2004. *Terrorists or Freedom Fighters: Reflections on the Liberation of Animals*. New York: Lantern Books.

Bettelheim, Bruno. 1980. "The Holocaust: One Generation Later." *Surviving and Other Essays*. New York: Vintage Press.

Breitman, Richard. 1998. *Official Secrets: What the Nazis Planned, What the British and Americans Knew*. New York: Hill and Wang.

Bretall, Robert, ed. 1936. *A Kierkegaard Anthology*. New York: The Modern Library. 339–371.

Brown, Dee. 1970. *Bury My Heart at Wounded Knee: An Indian History of the American West*. New York: Henry Holt and Company.

Burruss, Robert. 1993. "The Future of Eggs." *Baltimore Sun* 29 December: 16A. Cited in Davis 1996, 23–24.

Butler, Virgil. 2003. "Employee Describes Deliberate Torture of Chickens at Tyson Slaughter Plant." Poultry Press Vol. 13, No. 1 (Spring): 10–12.

Butler, Virgil, and Laura Alexander. 2004. "'Slaughterhouse Worker Turned Activist': UPC Talks with Virgil Butler and Laura Alexander." *Poultry Press* Vol. 14, No. 3 (Fall): 1–4. www.upc-online.org/slaughter.

Callicott, J. Baird. 1980. "Animal Liberation: A Triangular Affair." *Environmental Ethics* Vol. 2: 311–338.

Chapple, Christopher. 1986. "Noninjury to Animals: Jaina and Buddhist Perspectives." *Animal Sacrifices: Religious Perspectives on the Use of Animals in Science*. Ed. Tom Regan. Philadelphia: Temple University Press. 213–235.

Churchill, Ward. 1997. *A Little Matter of Genocide: Holocaust and Denial in the Americas 1492 to the Present*. San Francisco: City Lights Books.
_____. 2004. Foreword. "Illuminating the Philosophy and Methods of Animal Liberation." *Terrorists or Freedom Fighters: Reflections on the Liberation of Animals*. Ed. Steven Best and Anthony J. Nocella II. New York: Lantern Books.

Clark, Dustan, et al., 2004. "Understanding and Control of Gangrenous Dermatitis in Poultry Houses." University of Arkansas Cooperative Extension Service. www.thepoultrysite.com/FeaturedArticle/FATopic.asp?Display=173.

Coats, C. David. 1989. *Old MacDonald's Factory Farm: The Myth of the Traditional Farm and the Shocking Truth about Animal Suffering in Today's Agribusiness*. New York: Continuum.

Coetzee, J. M. 1999. *The Lives of Animals*. Princeton, NJ: Princeton University Press.

Coon, Craig. 1994. Telephone communication to Karen Davis, 25 July. Cited in Davis 1996: 135, 171 note 33.

Davis, Karen. 1989. "What's Wrong with Pain Anyway?" *The Animals' Agenda* February: 50–51.
_____. 1995–1996. "Expanding the Great Ape Project." *Poultry Press* Vol. 5, No. 4 (Fall/Winter): 2–3.
_____. 1996. *Prisoned Chickens, Poisoned Eggs: An Inside Look at the Modern Poultry Industry*. Summertown, TN: Book Publishing Company.
_____. 2001a. *More Than a Meal: The Turkey in History, Myth, Ritual, and Reality*. New York: Lantern Books.
_____. 2001b. "An Open Letter to *Vegan Voice*," December 26. (http://www.upc-online.org/011226vegan_voice_singer.html) Published in *Vegan Voice* 2002 (NSW, Australia) No. 9 (March-May): 17.
_____. 2002. "Review of *Eternal Treblinka: Our Treatment of Animals and*

the Holocaust, by Charles Patterson." *Poultry Press* Vol. 12, No. 2 (Summer): 8–10. www.upc-online.org/summer2002/etreview.html.
_____. 2003. "The Experimental Use of Chickens and Other Birds in Biomedical and Agricultural Research." United Poultry Concerns. www.upc-online.org/genetic/experimental.htm.
_____. 2004a. "Open Rescues: Putting a Face on Liberation." *Terrorists or Freedom Fighters? A Reflection on the Liberation of Animals*. Ed. Steven Best and Anthony J. Nocella, II. New York: Lantern Books. 195–212.
_____. 2004b. Letter. *Journal of the American Veterinary Medical Association* 1 July: 30.
_____. 2004c. "The Life of One Battery Hen." *AV Magazine* Vol. 112, No. 3 (Summer): 7–9. American Anti-Vivisection Society.
_____. 2005. "A Tale of Two Holocausts." *Animal Liberation Philosophy and Policy Studies Journal* Vol. 2, No. 2. Center on Animal Liberation Affairs (CALA). www.cala-online.org.
Dawkins, Marian Stamp. 1985. "The Scientific Basis for Assessing Suffering in Animals." *In Defense of Animals*. Ed. Peter Singer. New York: Basil Blackwell. 27–40.
DawnWatch. 10 May 2004. www.DawnWatch.com.
"Death, Nerve Damage Seen in Chickens Given DEET/Pyridostigmine." 1995. *Pesticide & Toxic Chemical News* 12 April: 36.
Dekkers, Midas. 1994. *Dearest Pet: On Bestiality*. Trans. Paul Vincent. New York: Verso.
Donovan, Josephine, and Carol J. Adams. 1996. *Beyond Animal Rights: A Feminist Caring Ethic for the Treatment of Animals*. New York: Continuum.
Druce, Clare. 2004. *Minny's Dream*. Cambridge, England: Nightingale Books.
Dunayer, Joan. 2001. *Animal Equality: Language and Liberation*. Derwood, MD: Ryce Publishing.
_____. 2004. *Speciesism*. Ibid.
Duncan, Ian. 2001. "Welfare Problems of Meat-type Chickens." Farmed Animal Well-Being Conference at the University of California-Davis June 28–29. *Poultry Press* Vol. 11, No. 3 (Fall): 1–2. www.upc-online.org/fall2001/well-being_conference_Review.html.
Espinosa, Jr., Peter B. (CKE Restaurants) 2002. Letter to Lauren (Ornelas) Sullivan. 25 January.
Etches, Robert. 1994. "Beyond Freezing Semen." First International Symposium on the Artificial Insemination of Poultry. University of Maryland, College Park, MD: 17–19 June.
Evans, E.P. 1998 (1906). *The Criminal Prosecution and Capital Punishment of Animals*. Union, New Jersey: The Lawbook Exchange, Ltd.
Friedlander, Albert H., ed. 1976. *Out of the Whirlwind: A Reader of Holocaust Literature*. New York: Schocken Books.
Goodman, Ellen. 1992. "The Seasonal Equivalent of Quality Time. *Baltimore Sun* 26 November: 31A.
Goodwin, Jan. 2004. *Nation* 8 March: 18–22.
Gray, Jason. 2003. "The Snow Leopard in the MetroToronto Zoo." *And We the Creatures*. Ed. C. J. Sage. San Jose, CA: Dream Horse Press.

Greger, Michael. 2003. "SARS: Another Deadly Virus From the Meat Industry" 13 April. www.veganMD.org; www.upc-online.org/poultry_diseases/sars.htm.

Guillermo, Kathy. 2005. "Response to Nathan Snaza's '(Im)possible Witness: Viewing PETA's "Holocaust on Your Plate."'" *Animal Liberation Philosophy and Policy Studies Journal* Vol. 2, No. 2.

Harris, Thomas. 1988. *The Silence of the Lambs.* New York: St. Martin's Press.

Henderson, Diedtra. 2004. "Bird-Flu Stirs Flurry of Precautions in US" *Denver Post* 15 February.

Howitt, William. 1844. *The Rural Life of England,* 3rd ed. London: Longman, Brown, Green, and Longmans.

HSUS (The Humane Society of the United States). 2004. "HSUS Says Burger King's Latest Promotion Leaves a Bad Taste." News release 21 October.

Hyland, J. R. 2000. *God's Covenant with Animals: A Biblical Basis for the Humane Treatment of All Creatures.* New York: Lantern Books.

Jacobs, Andrea. 2003. "PETA's 'Holocaust on Your Plate' campaign hits Denver," *Intermountain Jewish News* 22 August.

Jones, Pattrice. 2004. "Mothers with Monkeywrenches: Feminist Imperatives and the ALF." *Terrorists or Freedom Fighters: Reflections on the Liberation of Animals.* Ed. Steven Best and Anthony J. Nocella II. New York: Lantern Books. 137–156.

Jones, Tamara. 1999. "For the Birds." *The Washington Post*, 14 November: F1, F4–F5.

Judt, Tony. 2005. "Goodbye to All That?" *The Nation* 3 January: 15–18.

Kahn, Richard. 2004. Email communication to Karen Davis, 15 February.

Kalechofsky, Roberta, ed. 1995. Introduction. *Rabbis and Vegetarianism: An Evolving Tradition.* Marblehead, Massachusetts: Micah Publications.

_____. 2003. *Animal Suffering and the Holocaust: The Problem with Comparisons.* Marblehead, Massachusetts: Micah Publications.

Klug, Brian. 2004. "The Myth of the New Anti-Semitism." *The Nation* 2 February: 23–29.

Lal, Basant K. 1986. "Hindu Perspectives on the Use of Animals in Science." *Animal Sacrifices: Religious Perspectives on the Use of Animals in Science.* Ed. Tom Regan. Philadelphia: Temple University Press. 1990. 199–212.

Lane, Terry. 2003. "The Live Trade Must Stop." *The Age* (Melbourne, Australia) 28 September.

Langer, Ellen. 1989. *Mindfulness.* Reading, MA: Addison-Wesley Publishing Company. Cited in Schnurer, 108, 124 note 5.

Lapham, Lewis H. 2004. "Notebook: Revised text." *Harper's Magazine* Summer: 9–11.

Lemkin, Raphael. 1944. *Axis Rule in Occupied Europe: Laws of Occupation, Analysis of Government, Proposals for Redress.* Washington, DC: Carnegie Endowment for International Peace.

Lerner, Michael. 2003. *Healing Israel/Palestine: A Path to Peace and Reconciliation.* San Francisco: Tikkun Books.

Lifton, Robert Jay. 1986. *The Nazi Doctors: Medical Killing and the Psychology of Genocide*. New York: Basic Books.

Linzey, Andrew. 1986. "The Place of Animals in Creation: A Christian View." *Animal Sacrifices: Religious Perspectives on the Use of Animals in Science*. Ed. Tom Regan. Philadelphia: Temple University Press. 115–148.

Lorenz, Konrad. 1980. "Animals Have Feelings." *Der Spiegel* No. 47. Trans. E.M. Robinson. Cited in Davis 1996, 55.

Luke, Brian. 1996. "Justice, Caring, and Animal Liberation." *Beyond Animal Rights: A Feminist Caring Ethic for the Treatment of Animals*. Ed. Josephine Donovan and Carol J. Adams. New York: Continuum. 77–102.

MacKenzie, Debora, et al. 2003. "Killer Pneumonia Virus Linked to Birds." *New Scientist* 3 April. www.newscientist.com.

Mark, Patty. 2001. "To Free a Hen." *The Animals' Agenda* Vol. 21, No. 4 (July–August): 25–26. Cited in Davis 2004a, 204.

Mason, Jim. 1993. *An Unnatural Order: Uncovering the Roots of Our Domination of Nature and Each Other*. New York: Simon & Schuster. Rpt. Lantern Books, 2005.

Masson, Jeffrey Moussaieff. 2003. *The Pig Who Sang to the Moon: The Emotional World of Farm Animals*. New York: Ballantine Books.

MDA (Maryland Department of Agriculture). 2004. "Maryland Department of Agriculture Official News Release." 6 March.

Mench, Joy. 2001. "Welfare Problems of Laying Hens." Farm Animal Well-Being Conference at the University of California-Davis June 28–29. *Poultry Press* Vol. 11, No. 3 (Fall): 1–2. www.upc-online.org/fall/2001/well-being_conference_review.html.

Milgram, Stanley. 1974. *Obedience to Authority: An Experimental View*. New York: Harper & Row.

Mills, D. S., and C. J. Nicol. 1990. "Tonic immobility in spent hens after catching and transport." *Veterinary Record* Vol. 126 (3 March): 210–212. Cited in Davis 1996, 109–110.

Muhtadie, Luma. 2004. "Mass Slaughter of B.C. Fowl Ordered." *Globe and Mail* 5 April.

Munro, Estelle. (*Best Friends*) 2003. Email communication to Karen Davis, 1 May.

Myers. B. R. 2004. "Nasty, Brutish, and Short." *Atlantic Monthly* February: 115–118.

Noske, Barbara. 1989. *Humans and Other Animals: Beyond the Boundaries of Anthropology*. London: Pluto Press.

_____. 1993. "The Animal Question in Anthropology: A Commentary." *Society and Animals: Journal of Human and Animal Studies* Vol. 1, No. 2.

_____. 2004. "Two Movements and Human-Animal Continuity: Positions, Assumptions, Contradictions." *Animal Liberation Philosophy and Policy Studies Journal* Vol. 2, No. 1.

Oboler, Jeff. 2003. "A Torah Perspective on 'The Eternal Treblinka.'" Letter to Richard Schwartz.

O'Rourke, Kate. 2004. "The Animal Rights Struggle." *Journal of the American Veterinary Medical Association* 15 May: 1567–1568.

Orwell, George. "Marrakech." 1953 (1939). *Such, Such Were the Joys*. New York: Harcourt, Brace.

Patterson, Charles. 2002. *Eternal Treblinka: Our Treatment of Animals and the Holocaust*. New York: Lantern Books.

Paul-Murphy, Joanne, et al. 2004. "Veterinarians and Biomedical Researchers Agree Animals Feel Pain." *Animal Welfare Information Center Bulletin* Vol. 12. Nos. 1–2 (Summer): 9.

Peguri, Alfredo, and Craig Coon. 1993. "Effect of Feather Coverage and Temperature on Layer Performance." *Poultry Science* Vol. 72: 1318–1329.

Petrie, Jon. 2004. "Jon Petrie investigates the etymology of the word 'Holocaust.'" http://www.fpp.co.uk/Auschwitz/docs/Holocaust Usage.html. 6 February.

Phelps. Norm. 2002. *The Dominion of Love: Animal Rights According to the Bible*. New York: Lantern Books.

Plath, Sylvia. 1971. *The Bell Jar*. New York: Harper & Row.

Porphyry. 1965. *On Abstinence from Animal Food*. Trans. Thomas Taylor. Ed. Esme Wynne-Tyson. London & Fontwell: Centaur Press Ltd.

Prescott, Matt. 2003a. "Giant Graphic Display Shows How Today's Victims Languish in Nazi-Like Concentration Camps." News release 3 April. www.peta.org/mc/NewsItem.asp?id=2106.

_____. 2003b. Email communication to Karen Davis, 12 September.

_____. 2004. Email communication to Barbara Lorincz, 19 February.

Primatt, Humphry. (1776). *The Duty of Mercy and the Sin of Cruelty to Brute Animals*. London.

Rauch, Jonathan. 2003. "The Forgotten Millions." *The Atlantic Monthly* December: 27–28.

Regan, Tom, ed. 1986. *Animal Sacrifices: Religious Perspectives and the Use of Animals in Science*. Philadelphia: Temple University Press.

Ritvo, Harriet. 1987. *The Animal Estate: The English and Other Creatures in the Victorian Age*. Cambridge, Massachusetts: Harvard University Press.

Roberts, Catherine. 1980. *Science, Animals, and Evolution: Reflections on Some Unrealized Potentials of Biology and Medicine*. Westport, Connecticut: Greenwood Press.

Rogers, Lesley J. 1995. *The Development of Brain and Behaviour in the Chicken*. Wallingford, Oxon (UK), Cab International.

Roland, D.A., et al. 1984. "Toxic Shock-Like Syndrome in Hens and Its Relationship to Shell-Less Eggs." *Poultry Science* Vol. 63: 791–797. See Davis 1996, 135–136.

Rosenberger, Jack. 2004. "Vegetarian Advocate: Isaac Bashevis Singer." *Satya* September: 28–29.

Rule, Ann. 1989 (1980). *The Stranger Beside Me*. New York: Signet.

Ryder, Richard D. 1989. *Animal Revolution: Changing Attitudes towards Speciesism*. Cambridge, Massachusetts: Basil Blackwell.

Sax, Boria. 2000. *Animals in the Third Reich: Pets, Scapegoats, and the Holocaust*. New York: Continuum.

Scarry, Elaine. 1985. *The Body in Pain: The Making and Unmaking of the World*. New York: Oxford University Press. Quoted in Carol J. Adams. "Caring About Suffering." *Beyond Animal Rights: A Feminist Caring Ethic for the Treatment of Animals*. 1996. Ed. Josephine Donovan and Carol J. Adams. New York: Continuum.

Schnurer, Maxwell. 2004. "At the Gates of Hell: The ALF and the Legacy of Holocaust Resistance." *Terrorists or Freedom Fighters: Reflections on the Liberation of Animals*. Ed. Steven Best and Anthony J. Nocella II. New York: Lantern Books. 106–127.

Schochet, Elijah Judah. 1984. *Animal Life in Jewish Tradition: Attitudes and Relationships*. New York: Ktav Publishing House.

Schwartz, Richard H. 2001. *Judaism and Vegetarianism*. New York: Lantern Books.

Scully, Matthew. 2002. *Dominion: The Power of Man, the Suffering of Animals, and the Call to Mercy*. New York: St. Martin's Press.

Sebo, Jeff. 2005. "A Critique of the Kantian Theory of Indirect Duties to Animals." *Animal Liberation Philosophy and Policy Studies Journal* Vol. 2, No. 2.

Shenker, Israel. 1991. "The Man Who Talked Back to God: Isaac Bashevis Singer, 1904–91." *The New York Times Book Review* August 11: 11.

Singer, Isaac Bashevis. 1982 (1935). "The Letter Writer." *The Collected Stories*. New York: Farrar, Straus and Giroux. 250–276.

_____. "The Slaughterer." Ibid. 207–216.

Singer, Peter. 1990 (1975). *Animal Liberation*. New York: Avon Books.

_____. 1994. *Rethinking Life and Death: The Collapse of Our Traditional Ethics*. New York: St. Martin's Press.

_____. 2000. *Writings on an Ethical Life*. New York: HarperCollins.

_____. 2001. "Heavy Petting." www.nerve.com. March.

_____. 2002. "Book Review: *Animal Equality: Language and Liberty* by Joan Dunayer." *Vegan Voice* (NSW, Australia) No. 8 (Dec.–Feb.): 36.

Slouka, Mark. 2002. "A Year Later: Notes on America's Intimations of Mortality." *Harper's Magazine* September: 35–43.

Smith, Page, and Charles Daniel. 2000 (1975). *The Chicken Book*. Athens, GA: University of Georgia Press.

Snaza, Nathan. 2004. "(Im)possible Witness: Viewing PETA's 'Holocaust On Your Plate.'" *Animal Liberation Philosophy and Policy Studies Journal* Vol. 2. No. 1.

Sontag, Susan. 2003. *Regarding the Pain of Others*. New York: Farrar, Straus and Giroux.

Specter, Michael. 2003. "The Extremist." *New Yorker* 14 April: 52–67.

Stanley-Branscum, Doll. 1995. "Rescuing 'Layers.'" *Poultry Press* Vol. 5, No. 2 (Spring-Summer): 3–4. www.upc-online.org/rescuing.html.

Stern, Howard. 2002; 2004. *The Howard Stern Show* (Radio): 10 April; 27 August.

Superintendent of Belchertown State School v. Saikewicz, 373 Mass. 728,370 N.E.2d 417 (1977).

Swanson, Janice. 2002. "Why You Should Care About Animal Welfare." American Meat Institute Foundation Annual Animal Handling and Stunning Conference. 21–22 February.

Teale, Edwin Way, ed. 1954. *The Wilderness World of John Muir*. Boston: Houghton Mifflin.

Traverso, Enzo. 2003. *The Origins of Nazi Violence*. Trans. Janet Lloyd. New York: The New Press.

UPC (United Poultry Concerns). 2003. *Poultry Slaughter: The Need for Legislation*. www.upc-online.org/slaughter/slaughter3web.pdf.

_____. 2004a. www.upc-online.org/slaughter/.

_____. 2004b. *Inside a Live Poultry Market*. Video (VHS, DVD).

_____. 2004–2005. "'Inside a Live Poultry Market' Investigation in the Bronx Shows Misery, Sickness, Filth." *Poultry Press* Vol. 14, No. 4 (Winter): 4–5. http://www.upc-online.org/winter0405/market.htm.

Vaughan, Claudette. 2002. "Is This a Dangerous Philosopher?" *Vegan Voice* (NSW Australia) December–February: 7–8, 35.

Watts, Michael. 2002. "The Age of the Chicken." The Chicken: Its Biological, Social, Cultural, and Industrial History: An International Conference May 17–19. Yale University.

Weiss, Rick. 2005. "Bird Brains Get Some New Names, And New Respect." *The Washington Post* February 1: A10. www.upc-online.org/alerts/20105post.htm.

Wemelsfelder, F. 1991. "Animal Boredom: Do Animals Miss Being Alert and Active?" *Applied Animal Behaviour: Past, Present and Future: Proceedings of the International Congress Edinburgh 1991*. Ed. M.C. Appleby, et al. UK: Universities Federation for Animal Welfare. 120–123.

Wenig, Gaby. 2003. "Humane Atonement or Animal Cruelty?" *Jewish Journal of Greater Los Angeles* 30 October.

Wiesel, Elie. 1999. "The Perils of Indifference." 12 April. www.american-rhetoric.com/speeches/ewieselperilsofindifference.html.

"Wolves and Poodles." *Earth First!* March–April 2005. 31.

Young, James E. 1988. *Writing and Rewriting the Holocaust: Narrative and the Consequences of Interpretation*. Bloomington: Indiana University Press.

Index

About the Author

Karen Davis, Ph.D., is the founder and President of United Poultry Concerns (www.upc-online.org), a nonprofit organization that promotes the compassionate and respectful treatment of domestic fowl. She is the author of *Prisoned Chickens, Poisoned Eggs: An Inside Look at the Modern Poultry Industry; A Home for Henny; More Than a Meal: The Turkey in History, Myth, Ritual, and Reality;* and *Instead of Chicken, Instead of Turkey: A Poultryless "Poultry" Potpourri* (a cookbook). Karen is the editor of *Poultry Press*, the quarterly magazine of United Poultry Concerns. She maintains a sanctuary for rescued chickens and other domestic fowl in Machipongo, Virginia.

Of Related Interest from Lantern Books

Eternal Treblinka
Our Treatment of Animals and the Holocaust
Charles Patterson

"Charles Patterson's book will go a long way towards righting the terrible wrongs that human beings, throughout history, have perpetrated on non-human animals. I urge you to read it and think deeply about its important message."—**Jane Goodall**

More Than a Meal
The Turkey in History, Myth, Ritual, and Reality
Karen Davis

"Karen Davis shines a new light on the unfortunate, much-maligned bird that is the center of America's Thanksgiving ritual, and thereby illuminates the lies and hypocrisy that surround our eating habits and our attitudes to animals. *More Than a Meal* challenges all Americans to think about the values they want their annual family ritual to embody."—**Peter Singer**, DeCamp Professor of Bioethics, Princeton University; author, *Animal Liberation*

Animal Equality
Language and Liberation
Joan Dunayer

"Brilliant and devastating. *Animal Equality* is a book of monumental importance for animal rights. A tour de force that has no equal, it documents the cruelty to which nonhuman animals are routinely subjected and shows that speciesism pervades our language."—**Tom Regan**, author of *The Case for Animal Rights*

Speciesism
Joan Dunayer

"In this unique and impressive book, Joan Dunayer forcefully develops the most rigorous and consistent definition of speciesism ever offered. She also advances, in significant ways, the case for regarding sentience as the only criterion for possessing basic rights."—**Michael A. Fox**, Professor of Philosophy, Queen's University and author of *Deep Vegetarianism*

Terrorists or Freedom Fighters?
Reflections on the Liberation of Animals
Steven Best and Anthony J. Nocella, Jr., Editors

"Finally, a serious look at the latest liberation movement from both a historical, philosophical and activist perspective. Regardless of what one thinks about the tactics of the Animal Liberation Front, this long overdue book is a must-read for anyone concerned about the future of the movement for animal liberation."—**Michael Greger, MD**, Chief BSE Investigator for Farm Sanctuary, Mad Cow Coordinator for the Organic Consumers Association

An Unnatural Order
The Roots of Our Destruction of Nature
Jim Mason

"An eloquent, important plea for a total rethinking of our relationship to the animal world. Mason analyzes the West's 'dominionist' worldview, which exalts humans as overlords and owners of other life.... His powerfully argued manifesto will change many readers' attitudes toward hamburgers, animal experimentation, hunting, and circuses."—*Publishers Weekly*

Printed in the United States
81784LV00001B/1-150